PRIVATE EYE ANNUAL 2013

EDITED BY IAN HISLOP

"Good point, well made"

Published in Great Britain by
Private Eye Productions Ltd
6 Carlisle Street, London W1D 3BN
www.private-eye.co.uk

© 2013 Pressdram Ltd
ISBN 978-1-901784-60-2
Designed by Bridget Tisdall
Printed and bound in Great Britain by
Butler Tanner & Dennis, Frome, Somerset
2 4 6 8 10 9 7 5 3 1

PRIVATE EYE ANNUAL 2013

EDITED BY IAN HISLOP

"Isn't that dress a bit revealing?"

Nursery Times

The Paedo Piper – 'We Had No Idea'

by Our Conscience Staff
Jiminy Fixit

THE town of Hamelin was in a state of shock last night when it was revealed that the much-loved late Paedo Piper had, in fact, been a paedophile.

The Piper was well known for his eccentric multi-coloured clothing and love of popular music.

He was, however, an enigmatic figure, drifting in and out of town as the fancy took him.

He first came to people's attention as a sort of Mr Fix-it and when the Mayor wrote to him asking if the Piper could fix it for him to rid the town of rats, he duly obliged.

When he had completed the task he merely said, "How's about that then?" The grateful townspeople showered him with praise and he became a national treasure.

Piper's Travels

He subsequently developed an interest in the town's children and took them out for a day trip with the promise of some "wonderful tunes for the guys and gals".

Incredibly, none of the townspeople became remotely suspicious when none of the children ever returned.

Even when he said, "Yes, I'm the Paedo Piper. I've taken the children away never to return them," people merely thought he was joking.

"It's just the Piper being his normal paedo self," they said.

Now he is dead, at last the truth has emerged and a shocked populace are left asking themselves, "Why did we not listen to all those girls or boys or even the Brothers Grimm?"

On other pages

● *Prince Charmless's secret letters to minister: "That appalling gingerbread house should be made out of organic Duchy Original biscuits"* **2**

● *Trolls target Billy Goat's kid: "You're fat and look like a goat"* **3**

● *Stunt cow breaks sound barrier on return from moon jump* **94**

DAILY EXPRESS

FRIDAY SEPTEMBER 21, 2012

CORGI 'WAS MURDERED'

By Our Conspiracy Staff **DAVID ICKE**

THE supposed "death from natural causes" of the Royal corgi Monty was nothing of the sort, we can exclusively reveal.

According to one highly placed source, "Monty was fuggin' murdered! He was run over by a white Fiat Uno driven by that fuggin' murderer the Duke of fuggin' Edinburgh."

The anonymous source (M. Fugger) went on to accuse the palace of a deliberate cover-up which (cont. p. 94)

UK Lawyers Demand Removal of 'Offensive Cross Symbol'

BY OUR LEGAL STAFF JOSHUA ROSENBEARD

A TEAM of British government lawyers yesterday argued before the European Court of Human Rights that the "displaying of a cross in public" was so offensive to non-Christians that the UK authorities should be allowed to ban such practices entirely.

They cited as the most offensive example of this "religious bigotry" the use of the cross symbol in the so-called "Union Flag".

The lawyers claimed that to make the national flag acceptable, the red "cross of St George" should be removed from the design, as not only carrying offensive religious connotations but as an incitement to racial hatred at times of heightened tension (ie, international football competitions).

The lawyers went on to argue that equally unacceptable was the red "cross of St Patrick", which was not only a further offensive religious symbol, but was also an insensitive and outmoded memorial to 800 years of British imperialism in Ireland.

Concluding their case after 12 agreeable days spent in Strasbourg,

Offensive old flag | **Inoffensive new flag**

at the expense of the British taxpayer, the lawyers finally urged that the remaining part of the flag consisted only of the so-called "saltire" or the white cross of St Andrew on a blue background.

This, they pointed out, was not only offensive on religious grounds, but it would also be quite absurd for the stripped down UK flag to be identical with that of a future independent Scotland.

"The only rational solution to these illegalities," argued Sir Simon Hugefee for the government's legal team, "must be to remove all three of these provocative religious symbols from the design, leaving a white flag."

This new-look Union Jack, he suggested, could then be waved in any future dispute with the EU – or indeed anyone else.

"Having a two-second memory doesn't matter anymore"

Monday

As the not inconsiderably successful Olympic and Paralympic Games came to an end, I was looking forward in no small measure to reading how the key to Team GB's amazing success was the funding provided to our victorious athletes by the National Lottery which, of course, was my idea and my most lasting achievement.

At breakfast this morning, as I was eating my bowl of Golden Wiggo's, I asked my wife Norman, who was reading the Daily Mail, "Is there by any chance any reference to my own contribution to national life in that excellent newspaper?"

Norman gave me a rather odd in my judgement look and replied, "There is a great deal about you. You are mentioned 28 times in one article."

"That is indeed very gratifying," I said. "At last it seems that the Voice of Middle England has recognised my legacy to this country."

"Yes," said Norman, tipping my bowl of cereal over my head. "You are remembered as the man in grey underpants who had an affair with that Currie woman who has just spilled the beans again over twelve pages of this appalling newspaper. The only Olympics you seem to have had any connection with are of the bedroom variety."

This was not, in my opinion, either clever or funny. Oh no.

"Am I sick of the Olympic legacy..."

MACCA AWARDED THE LEGION D'HONNEUR

That President Hollande Citation In Full

Alors! Salut! Félicitations! La France dit bienvenue à Sir Paul McCartney aussi connu universellement sous le nom Macca, chanteur célèbre des hit songs énormes par example "Hiersterday", "Moules de Kintyre," et "Na, Na Na, NaNaNaNa", sur behalf de notre grande pays, moi, President Hollande, pas forgetting ma très belle partner Mme Rottweiler, donnez-vous the Legion d'Honneur pour votre contribution magnifique au monde de la pop juste comme le grand socialiste Harold Wilson a fait quand il était un peu desperate pour de bonne publicité comme moi... er… Maintenant vous standez alongside les grandes noms historiques e.g. Marcel Marceau, Hector Berlioz et Jean-Paul Sartre.

© Government Socialist Français

"Matthew... that side is for the artists"

The world's top female academic, Harvard Professor Deirdre Spart, sets out the definitive proof that the 4th Century papyrus fragment  portraying Jesus as married *must* have been authentic.

Ten Tell-Tale Signs That Prove Jesus Was Married

1. Hopeless at shopping (too few loaves and fishes)
2. Amateur carpenter (doing DIY)
3. Never seen smiling
4. Carried weight of world on shoulders
5. Knocked tables over, causing mess for others to clean up
6. Spent last night out with mates
7. Told same old parables again and again
8. Thought he was God's gift

(That's enough of this).

PLUS **Cut-Out-'N'-Send Free Complaint Form**

Dear Sir,

You are pathetic hypocrites. You wouldn't run this piece about Mohammed, would you?

Signed _____

No. Ed.

DRAWING ALL FAITHS TOGETHER

Hi!

The one thing I really feel I can contribute on this earth is my gift for bringing together people of different persuasions and beliefs.

That is how I brought peace to Northern Ireland. That is how I am bringing peace to the Middle East.

And that is how I managed to bring together round the table the managements of two of the most significant international corporations in the world.

Everyone said there was no way in a million years that these two implacable enemies could be made to agree on a deal – the world-famous mining company Excreta and the even more respected commodities trader Greedcorps.

These two great companies were at each other's throats. The planned merger between them seemed completely off the table.

But they called in the only man in the world who might be able to pull off a genuine miracle – namely, the Rev. Tony Blair!

After just three hours in Claridge's I had talked the bosses of the two companies into a totally different frame of mind.

Greedcore's top man, Ivan the Terribleburger, and his opposite number at Excreta, my old friend, Sheikh Shufti al Bakhanda, were happily shaking hands on an incredible agreement – ie, they agreed to give me $1 million for having pulled off what everyone had thought was impossible.

I know I abolished poverty in Africa – but that was child's play compared with bringing together two of the richest and most powerful men in the world, by persuading them that, for all their apparent differences, they in fact shared one core belief which transcends everything else, a belief which I myself totally share – namely that there is no higher calling in this world than to make huge amounts of money.

I tell you, being able to help mankind in this way makes you feel like a million dollars!!!

Yours,

Rev. T. Blair

(former vicar of St. Albion's, Currently Chair and President-for-life of the DAFT Foundation – Drawing All Financiers Together)

"Good evening and welcome to 'Strictly No Dancing'..."

KATE TOPLESS PHOTOS: LATEST

Get your writs out, darling!

"We hired a photographer for the party to make all the guests feel like celebrities"

JUST A QUICK UPSKIRT SHOT LOVE

👑 INGRID SEWAGE

An open letter to Kate Middleton from the distinguished editor of "Royalties" magazine

Kate, what were you thinking of when you took off your bikini top in full public view of a photographer hiding in a tree only a thousand metres away?

You must have been insane to be so reckless as to expose yourself so publicly in a private chateau miles from anywhere! Whatever next? Are you going to take off your clothes to get in the bath without checking whether a passing spy satellite is within range of your bathroom window? Are you going to bring down the entire monarchy by your frankly careless exhibitionism?

No Kate, you are in a unique position as our future queen and you must remember never to do anything private ever again and that includes going to the toilet.

© Ingrid Sewage 2012

DIRTY DES – The Comic Strip

I WOULD NEVER HAVE RUN THOSE PICTURES OF KATE...

...THEY'RE NOWHERE NEAR FILTHY ENOUGH!!

CHANNEL X

TOTALLY NAKED ROYAL EXPOSED

IN AN extraordinary twist to the Kate Middleton saga, a leading member of the Royal Family has been found wearing no clothes at all.

Richard III has been discovered in a car park in Leicester wearing "absolutely nothing".

Onlookers said, "We were shocked when we realised that a respected king like Richard III was lying around in a public place without a single shred of any garment. He didn't even have a codpiece to hide his modesty."

A spokesman for Richard III told reporters, "The late king is absolutely furious at this invasion of the privacy of his grave. To be quite frank, he's got the hump."

THE USELESS SIMON

Polly Filler's long-suffering partner is given his own column

HOW could we useless menfolk have got it so spectacularly wrong? There we were thinking that women wanted respect, equality, consideration and occasional help loading the dishwasher, when actually what they all want is domination, spanking, bondage and nipple clamps. For any martians out there, I'm talking, of course, about Fifty Shades of Grey or Fifty Million Sales A Day, as I amusingly called it when discussing the new literary phenomenon with the lads after the five-a-side footie, when we were all watching Jeremy Clarkson's Extreme Monster Truck Racing on Dave Ja Vu 3 Gold with a couple of beers!

Why did we bother with all that trying to be sensitive and caring and sharing when we could have just chained the little ladies to the door knob and whacked them on the bum with a cricket bat!

Fifty Shades of Gray-Nicolls, as I said to the lads after we'd been to the T20 cricket at Lords and we were watching England give Moldova Reserves a drubbing on EuroSkySport 7 on the plasma TV in the Slug and Piano on Chiswick High Street!

Ok, Ms E.L. James or Ms E.L. Shames, as I quipped to our toddler Charlie when I was helpfully doing some holiday childcare by taking him along to the afternoon screening of The Expendables II, so that his mum, Polly, could finish off a column, or a bottle of Chardonnay more like it... er... where was I?

ANYWAY, it's no more Mr Nice Guy from yours truly. No more Useful Simon, putting out the recycling, picking up my own underpants from the bathroom floor and asking La Filler how her day was!

Oh no. From now on, the Useless Simon is going to behave like a complete bastard, turn Polly's study into a room of pain and try out some of these new fancy S&M moves!

So watch out, our new au pair, Fru Tee, from Taiwan. I've got a rolled up copy of Nuts magazine, which is swishing your way!

Fifty Shedloads of Wahey, as I said to the lads after (cont. p. 94)

©Useless Simon 2012.

The Amazing New iPhone 5 – Your Questions Answered

Q: In what way is the amazing new iPhone 5 different from the amazing iPhone 4?

A: It's more expensive.

Exclusive to all newspapers
An Apology: The Police

IN RECENT weeks, we, in common with all other newspapers, may have given the impression that Britain's police were a thoroughly dishonest, untrustworthy bunch of corrupt, self-seeking time-servers, ready to stop at nothing in their efforts to cover up their own failings and guilty of leaking false stories to the media. Headlines such as "Hillsborough cover-up shows police are incapable of telling the truth", "Jail is too good for Hillsborough coppers" and "string up the lying Hillsborough chief plod" might have led readers to believe that the police were in some way less than paragons of public service who had the complete confidence of a grateful nation.

We now realise, in light of the contrasting versions we have been given of recent events involving Mr Andrew Mitchell and the police on duty in Downing Street, that when it comes to knowing who is more likely to be telling the truth – a policeman or a Conservative Cabinet Minister – the honest British bobby trying to do a difficult job in trying circumstances wins every time. We apologise to our readers for any confusion our earlier reports might have caused.

Boris Johnson Joins the Outcry Over Pleb-gate

A personal message from the Mayor

CRIPES! What on earth was Chummy Mitchell thinking of, using the word "pleb"? No wonder he was nearly arrested and, in my book, he jolly well should have been banged up in chokey for what was, after all, a pretty heinous offence, ie using a bastardisation of a perfectly good Latin word "plebeius".

Furthermore, before Master Mitchell leaps back in the saddle and pedals off to call the next honest copper "plebeius", he should remember to use the vocative case "plebei" since Mitchell Minor is clearly addressing a policeman (singular) directly and aiming his unfortunate remarks squarely at him.

If he can't get this right, then I'm afraid arresting him won't be sufficient and we will have to throw him to the lions – an example of "panem and circenses" that would be enjoyed by many of this country's plebeiis (ablative plural, in case Johnny Pedant is trying to catch old Bozza out).

PS (post scriptum): If there was a plebicite, guess who would come in primus well ahead of the pares?! No offence, Dave!

DEFICIT SLASHED TO RECORD HIGH

By Our Financial Staff **Owen Lotsamoney** and **Phil Blackhole**

THE Coalition's deficit secretary Francis Maude last night proudly announced that the government's cornerstone policy of reducing public debt was "delivering a brilliant success".

In August, he revealed, "We only had to borrow a mere £14.4 billion, which is only slightly more than we had to borrow in August last year and a vastly smaller amount than we've had to borrow every other month this year.

"So, you see, the August figure is actually a record, and I think that's something we can all be proud of.

"It shows that we are well on course to reducing the deficit to zero by the year 3012."

Dave Snooty AND HIS NEW PALS

S A L M A N
R U S H D I E

He gripped his legendary Mont Blanc fountain pen, the pen that had been his constant companion during those dark years of martyrdom, a martyrdom which, friends told him reassuringly, he had borne with exceptional grace, and began the arduous, heroic process of signing copy after copy of his memoir, which friends, including Bono, Simon Callow and Ian McEwan, had all insisted was a true masterpiece.

This was a lonely business, signing copies of his own memoir in a legendary bookshop crowded with readers anxious for his art and for his wisdom, readers who wished to hang on, like small animals – rabbits, puffins, hamsters, newts – to his every well-chosenish word.

He dutifully signed his own name with unrivalled intensity. He thought of other writers – Tolstoy, Conrad, the legendary Dostoevsky – who were now dead, but had once signed their own names with similar passion.

A new thought leapt into his head like a genie. Yes, he was half-remembering something Britney Spears had said to him at a party in Manhattan thrown by Martin Scorsese for Calista Flockhart on behalf of Tina Brown. Now what was it? Those cruel, ill-intentioned words came flooding back, like a great rush of water that creates something truly life-destroying, like a flood.

"I loved your last book, man."

Those words had hit him like daggers. How he had been hurt by that thoughtless sentence! There was probably not enough love in the world to heal him at that moment. How could someone be so dismissive of his earlier works? Spears was clearly implying, in her offhand, insolent way, that, at best, she had not read them. And what of his books that were still waiting to be written, the books still hatching in his powerful mind like hens that would one day blossom into majestic swans, floating on the sea of thought? Trapped in the prison of her own making, Britney Spears hadn't even bothered to ask after them.

How could this singer – now fat, and gone to seed – be so rude, so brutal, so shockingly unpleasant?

He felt the dark clouds loom above him, waiting to break.

He looked at the long line of customers stretching around the legendary bookshop like a magical glacier. Thankfully, he had never lost his capacity to come up with images like that, or so his friends told him, nor how to express them in a way which was wonderfully well-suited to their expression in every way.

All these customers were clutching copies of his memoir, which his true friends had already pronounced, with their customary intelligence, utterly magnificent.

Even in the exceptionally fraught circumstances of a book-signing, with queues of strangers desperate for the sustenance of his art, and all baying for his signature, he never lost his sense of humanity, his deep love for all mankind.

Life had taught him that, in his sixties, a man comes into his manhood. He felt substantial, grounded, strong. He was magnanimous in his dealings with those human beings who craved his signature, even if they were not well known, and would make a point of occasionally looking up in their direction for a few seconds as he handed them back his book.

He drew deep comfort from the thought of the pleasure it gave them to be greeted by such a world class writer in this way, and this gave him the strength to carry on.

As he signed his own name, over and over again, a manager asked him if he would like something to drink. It made him think of the drinks he had once enjoyed with Mario Vargas Llosa, Stephen Sondheim, Tina Brown, Harold Pinter, Bruce Forsyth, Anthea Turner, Susan Sontag and The Hitch at the legendary River Cafe where Ruthie Rogers, wife of the great architect Richard Rogers, had given him a heartwarming hug.

There was something about him that made women yearn to hug him, and regularly to offer him the mingled pleasures of their delightful bodies.

For all his wicked certainty, for all his rigid dogma, The Ayatollah had never have known the true pleasure of a hug from Antonia Byatt.

As told to C R A I G B R O W N

RUSHDIE FATWA MEMOIR

Body double hired (*just in case*)

THE TIMES ROMAN
—— 55 BC ——

Brutus Speech
Wows Conference

BY OUR POLITICAL STAFF **MARC ANTONY BEEVOR**

Rome, Tuesday

THE much-loved Senator, Brutus Johnson, was given a standing ovation by the mob yesterday as he made a barn-storming speech in support of his friend, the dictator Julius Cameron. "I come not to bury Caesar", he joked, "but to praise him."

The audience laughed uproariously at Brutus' humorous remarks about the man he called "Jules" and applauded his promise "not to stab Caesar in the back at the first opportunity".

ET TU BOJO?

Addressing rumours that he wished to stand for leader at a future date, possibly the Ides of March, Brutus told the cheering assembly, "You all know that Brutus is an honourable man. Ha, ha, ha."

Brutus then went on to praise himself for the brilliant organisation of the recent chariot races in the capital and said that what was needed in the country was a can-do spirit.

"Rome can be built in a day," he promised delighted supporters. He then ended his oration with a passionate plea, "Friends, Romans, Countrymen. Lend me your wives," and the crowd went (cont. *94 AD*)

WILD SCENES GREET NOBEL PEACE PRIZE DECISION

THE awarding of the Nobel Peace Prize to the EU quickly gave way to wild celebrations on the streets of Europe, from as far afield as Athens to Madrid.

In Athens, tens of thousands of masked youths, overwhelmed with pride, celebrated the decision by hurling Molotov cocktails at police who were mounting a ring of steel around the parliament building, whilst chanting Nazi slogans about the German Chancellor Angela Merkel.

Meanwhile, in Madrid, police using water cannon and stun grenades fought pitched battles with delighted Spaniards who had poured onto the streets to celebrate the momentous decision.

The President of the European Union, Herman Von Rumpoy, praised the Nobel committee for the decision, saying Europe was forever in its debt and would write off that debt with all the other money it owes sometime in 3089.

(Reuters)

"You forgot to take it off! Didn't the barber say anything?"

J.K. ROWLING

THEN	NOW

Children queue up to buy latest novel	Critics queue up to slag off latest novel

MILIBAND A GEEK IN POLITICS

Hands up who wishes I was my brother

The Eye's Controversial New Columnist

The columnist who kicks his blanket off eight times a night

This week I am angry about so-called criticisms of Ed Miliband's progress as leader of the Labour party after two years. Speaking from my great experience as a baby *(see photo)*, I think he has made excellent progress. From what I saw from his conference speech, at two years Mr

Miliband has learned how to walk up steps, recognise objects, say simple sentences using two or more words and use his imagination to create make-believe scenarios for himself and his friends. This is perfectly "normal" after two years, though granted I have never seen him kick a ball or carry out simple instructions, but not everybody progresses at the same rate. Perish the thought! I, of course, had an award-winning column at two, but only because I had a temper tantrum and wouldn't shut up until they gave *(cont. p. 94)*

"We should have a referendum on whether we need the gerundive"

IMF Warns That Austerity Causes Austerity

by U. Turner

THE International Monetary Fund has warned that the austerity cuts it said were essential if Britain and Europe were to escape economic meltdown, have caused an economic meltdown.

"Having studied the results of two years of austerity, we now conclude that austerity leads to austerity in the countries which implement it," said an IMF spokesman.

Downgrading its growth forecasts from "abandon all hope ye who enter here" to "bring out your dead", the IMF said that more austerity measures would be needed to combat the austerity measures that had led to austerity throughout the region.

"It's only through a fresh round of austerity that Britain and Europe can hope to escape from the misery caused by the first round of austerity."

Notes&queries

On American television, the Prime Minister didn't know the meaning of the term 'Magna Carta'. Does anyone know the answer to this obscure question?

● It is well known that Hollywood 'A'-lister Clint Eastwood was the first to utter the words, "It's a Magna Carta, punk. The most powerful constitutional treaty in the world" in the nearly-eponymous film "Get Carta, in which Clint played Dirty Henry ("Harry") de Bohun, the Earl of Hereford, establishing the rule of law in the mean streets of Runnymede.
The Rev M. Kermode.

● I hate to disagree with a cinema buff of the cloth, but the Rev. Kermode is hopelessly out of his depth. The Magna Carta, as all medieval historians know perfectly well, were ice cream wagons or carts (carta) which offered a large chocolate-based confection (a magnum) on a stick. The popularity of the Magna Carta provided at low cost by the rebellion united the country barons who were nostalgic for the glorious reign of the previous monarch Richard Coeur de Lyons (founder of the famous British ice cream company).
Professor H. Mantel.

Answers please:

Why did David Cameron go on a chat show? (Apart from to prepare the way for his US lecture tour once he is sacked?)

"Quick! Fetch our worst camera"

What's black and white and red all over?

You – after the cull

GOVERNMENT GIVES GO-AHEAD TO BURGLAR CULL

By Our Agricultural Staff **T.B. Vaccine**

THE Government today announced a controversial new policy of eliminating the burglar population by whatever means necessary.

Said a Government spokesman, "People have a romantic view of these feral creatures, with their characteristic black-and-white markings on their jerseys, but they really are vermin and a menace to the whole country."

Mr Grayling continued, "From now on, it will be acceptable to use what I call 'proportionately disproportional force', by which I mean bludgeoning them to death with a rolling pin, stabbing them with a kitchen knife, shooting them in the head with a sawn-off shotgun and, of course, gassing them in your oven."

Animal rights campaigners were quick to comment, exclaiming, "This is fine – it doesn't hurt any animals, just humans."

Brian May Not Like This

Burglar-lovers, however, were angry at the proposed cull, saying, "Burglars are some of Britain's best-loved creatures, roaming around at night, burrowing into your living room and taking your plasma TV whilst you're asleep. They should be left alone to get on with their lives. They are no danger to cattle – except for the ones that steal cattle, obviously."

The Adventures of Mr Milibean

Fountain & Jamieson

IT'S SUCH A RELIEF!

THANK HEAVENS THE BADGER CULL WAS POSTPONED AT THE VERY LAST MINUTE!

WHO'D HAVE THOUGHT, JUST WHEN THEY WERE ABOUT TO GET READY TO DO IT...

HE STARTED TO DO WELL AT PRIME MINISTER'S QUESTIONS!

HENRY DAVIES

The Alternative Rocky Horror Service Book

No. 94 The Solemnisation of Holy Matrimony (revised version)

The President (*for it is he, or she, or a person of transgender, or none of the above*): Hi, everyone. This is N and M's big day!

(Here he may name the couple as Simon and Rowena, or Barry and Chardonnay, or Charles and Simon, if the bishop isn't too fussed.)

I want you all to have a really great time.

All: Indeedy-doody!

(Or they may say "Way to go, Vicar", or whatever else comes to their mind)

The Introductory Address

The President: As you know, the Church has moved on from all that fuddy-duddy old "Marriage Service" stuff – so this new-style celebration is very much something for you all to make up as you go along. It's what we call the "C of E DIY wedding". So, N and M, I see you have decided to dress as Elvis Presley and Lara Croft, and to arrive at the church by parachute. That's a great start, but what do you want to do next?

The Decision

The President shall then present the bride and groom with a range of options as to how the service should proceed:

● *a recording of a popular song may here be played with the congregation invited to dance in the aisles*

or

● *there may be a reading from some suitable text, such as the autobiography of Ms Katie Price, The Hobbit by J.K. Tolkien or Professor Richard Dawkin's The Atheist Gene*

or

● *the couple may decide that they've had quite enough of this dreary church rubbish and that they just want to go off to the party straightaway.*

The Marriage

The President (*as the congregation heads for the door*): I now declare you husband and wife, partner and partner, Elvis and Lara, or whatever you guys feel comfortable with.

All (*having a fag in the churchyard*): Thanks, vicar.

The Dismissal

The President: Bless! Have a great day, and don't forget – we do funerals as well, and they're now just as informal, relaxed and fun as our weddings!

Modern last words

"I wish I'd made more friends on Facebook"

"Tell Al Gore... I tried!"

"Listen carefully. My passwords can all be found... urgh..."

INTERNATIONAL PARIAH INTERVIEWED ON CNN

HUMAN rights activists were outraged last night when one of the world's most hated men was given a prime time platform on American television. Piers Morgan was shown in a question-and-answer session with bland, mild-mannered, inof-fensive Iranian President Ahmadinejad.

Viewers phoned in with complaints, jamming the CNN switchboard (Mary Lou), with one complaining, "It's appalling. How could they make poor Mahmoud sit in the same room as that odious (cont. Channel 94)

TV Highlights

Nigelissima

UKIP's very own Nigel Farage stars in his unique show, cooking up an entirely non-European feast with only the most authentic British ingredients (no garlic). Watch him tantalise and tease the audience with such delicious delights as tonight's recipe – Traditional English Fruitcake!

ME AND MY SPOON

RHYS IFANS

Do you have a favourite spoon?

Fuck off. I'm bored with you now. Bored, bored, bored.

Mr Ifans' publicist writes: Rhys had a Lemsip shortly before the interview which may have unbalanced him slightly, causing him to slur his words and to experience some difficulty in remembering the name of the film he was meant to be plugging.

13

SAVILE SCANDAL GROWS

So, what's it like, working in the BBC?

SAVILE INVESTIGATION

by Our Showbiz Reporter **Jimmy So Vile**

POLICE leading the investigation into claims about Jimmy Savile have arrested the 1970s.

"We believe that the 1970s colluded with the stars of the day, like Savile, to carry out this abuse by being a totally different era from the modern day," said Inspector Knacker

"The 1970s would like us to think it was the decade of space hoppers, Spangles and chopper bikes, but we all now know this lovable façade was just there to allow heinous crimes to be committed."

Detective Knacker said he expected more decades could be arrested as the inquiry was widened

and also promised if the charges were proved, Jimmy Savile would be spending a very long time in prison.

Meanwhile, the BBC Director General George Entwistle has announced that in the wake of the Jimmy Savile paedophile scandal engulfing the broadcaster, the BBC is to close.

"With every passing day it becomes clearer that our defence that it was the work of one rogue editor is untenable," said the Director General, being chased down the street by ITV reporters.

BBC sources said the corporation would lay low for a few months and then reopen as the "BBC on Sunday".

'BBC CELEBRITY BEHAVED INAPPROPRIATELY WITH ME' Claims Money

by Our Financial Staff **Jeremy Taxman**

A LARGE pile of money came forward last night and accused a top BBC presenter of "abusing" the system by "grabbing" as much of the money as possible before the taxman could get his share of it.

Said a BBC spokesman, "It was all a different world back then, yesterday, and no one thought there was anything wrong with having a bit of hanky-panky with your finances. There was a different attitude to money –

certainly not everyone was a tax maniac."

The BBC, however, later said they would launch an immediate inquiry into how celebrities were allowed to get away with this disgraceful behaviour for so long.

TV HIGHLIGHTS

BBC1 Watchdog

● Consumer champion Anne Robinson looks into the dodgy world of TV

presenters who set up off-shore companies in order to avoid paying tax in the UK and names and shames herself.

'I WASN'T GROPED AT BBC' Says Woman

by Our History Staff **Hugh Trevor-Groper**

IN A shock confession last night, a female broadcaster admitted that she had never been assaulted by a male colleague during her time at the BBC.

She said, "It has taken me a long time to come forward because I feared for my career if everyone knew that nothing untoward had happened.

"But," she continued, "now that everyone else is getting their name in the paper I feel I must set the record straight.

"The truth is in my case there

was no groping, fondling or lewd suggestions whatsoever."

The BBC has launched an immediate inquiry and a spokesman for the Corporation announced, "This is well below the standard of behaviour we expect at the BBC and we must act at once to protect our hard-earned reputation for indecency."

SHOCKING 1979 EPISODE OF 'JIM'LL FIX IT' REVEALED

I'd like to screw every miner in Britain

I'm way ahead of you, Maggie

THOSE SAVILE PROGRAMMES IN FULL

1. Top of the Pervs Sir Jimmy reveals his greatest bits.

2. Clunk Click Sir Jimmy tells us about the importance of restraints when embarking on a ride.

3. This is the Age of the Teen Sir Jimmy extols the virtues of First Class (Class 1A, Duncroft School).

4. Jim'll F*** It Popular show where children are given a badge for allowing Sir Jimmy's dreams to come true.

FREDDIE STARR 'NEW ABUSE VICTIM COMES FORWARD'

BBC SAVILE SCANDAL — NET WIDENS

You look creepy

Trust me...
I'm on telly

BBC ABUSE CASE LATEST

by Our Media Staff
P.D. James-Savile

DETAILS have emerged of shocking and systematic abuse of the BBC by Rupert Murdoch. The abuse dates back to the closure of the News Of The World and has been linked to Mr Murdoch's unhealthy interest in taking over the entire media.

Mr Murdoch has a reputation for bullying and has used his position as the most powerful man in the world to assault the BBC whenever possible. There are now believed to be "hundreds of cases" where Mr Murdoch had attacked the BBC.

"People knew it was going on for years," said one insider, "but no one wanted to take him on. He was too influential and had friends in high places."

Said a spokesman for Mr Murdoch, "It was a long time ago and things were different then. He can't remember anything about it and *(we get the idea, Ed)*.

DAVE ROCK SPEAKS TO THE GNOME

Prior to his arrest next week, 70s rocker Dave Rock speaks frankly and movingly about the ordeal of appearing on Top of The Pops

Yeah, it was a mad and fantastic time, as I wrote in my autobiography *Lock up your Daughters*, and of course at the same time, as I said to the *Mail*, the *Telegraph* and *Nuts* magazine last week, it was really disgusting and reprehensible.

People gotta understand the 70s was a completely different world with completely different values, man, and even though it was a completely different world with completely different values, I never had no part of it, 'cos I knew one day forty years down the line I'd be asked about it.

TOTP was iffy, and made me uneasy deep down and my unease was so deep within my soul, it only resurfaced two weeks ago. But everyone knows I never let my girlfriend come on the set because of my deep seated unease, and I wouldn't stand for her cavorting with me and the lads until the early hours, certainly not on a school night. So anyway, I rang up Max Clifford and he *(cont. p. 94)*

"Sit"

BATTERSEA DOGS HOME

THE PEOPLE'S PERV

Schools and hospitals

Yes please!!!

NHS WAITING LIST SHOCK

THE failure of the NHS to treat the Savile scandal seriously has been justified by a senior Health spokesman:

"The delays of up to 40 years to get any attention for this story are in no way our fault.

"There is, unfortunately, a very long waiting list of people wanting to explain why Jimmy Savile was given a bed in a children's ward and given free rein to wander around hospitals in the middle of the night with no questions asked."

He continued, "It is very sad that these very old stories eventually died and *(cont. p. 94)*

HOW could the BBC's Director General possibly claim he didn't know what was going on?

This is a man who was supposed to be in charge of a huge media organisation and yet he says with a straight face that he had no idea what his staff were doing and then, even worse, denies covering up the whole sordid business?

Who does he think he is. James Murdoch? *(You're fired. R.M.)*.

FRESH ALLEGATIONS OF STARS PREYING ON VERY YOUNG WOMEN

But she told me she was over 50

"See you... oh, and by the way, you hold it the other way round"

WHAT YOU MISSED

 (All channels, all the time)

BBC interviewer: I have with me in the studio Dr Goodman, who is an expert on child abuse. Dr Goodman, this whole affair is very damaging for the BBC, isn't it?

Goodman: Well, it's most damaging of course for the victims who have had to live with...

Interviewer: I'm sorry to interrupt, but I must press you on the important question of the role of the BBC and, in particular, the future of the current Director General.

Goodman: The important question is, I think, how the perpetrators of this sort of crime were allowed...

Interviewer: With respect, Dr Goodman, you seem to be deliberately trying to steer the discussion away from the vital issue of the crisis at the BBC.

Goodman: I...

Interviewer: How do you explain, for example, the email from the Assistant Deputy Editor of Newsnight to the Deputy Assistant Head of News in reply to a statement by the Head of Vision when answering a blog written by...

Goodman: I'm sorry, I wanted to mention briefly those other institutions like the NHS where...

Interviewer: Look, John Simpson, the BBC World Affairs Editor, who is a pretty important BBC person, told BBC's Panorama that this BBC catastrophe was the single most important story in the history of the universe. And yet you are trying to... *(Cont. 94 Khz)*

Tonight on the BBC

9.00pm News
What will tonight's Panorama say about Newsnight?

10.00pm Panorama
Why is Newsnight in the news?

11.00pm Newsnight
What news about Newsnight was on Panorama?

12.00pm Late News
What did Newsnight say about Panorama's news about Newsnight?

For further coverage, see BBC Newsnight24.

Next week on the BBC: Children in Need – a whole evening devoted to children in need of rescuing from the BBC's Jimmy Savile.

NATION SHALL SPEAK PEACE UNTO NATION

Bastard!
Coward!
Paedo!
Perv!
Liar!
Bitch!
Traitor!

TRACEY IS A SLA...
POLICE

"I see myself as an opinion former, as social commentator, using whichever form of social media seems appropriate"

POLICE LOG

Neasden Central Police Station

0930 hrs All officers to attend post-Hillsborough training workshop. First module: the importance of not falsifying evidence in police notebooks, particularly if one is likely to be caught out 20 years later.

1015 hrs Armed response unit (PCs Barnet and Hainault) summoned to Asda Grove following reports that a suspect, dressed as a Jedi knight and armed with a deadly Star Wars-style light sabre, was running amok amongst shoppers in the new Mo Farah shopping precinct. Suspect was successfully brought down by a 50,000-volt charge from PC Hainault's taser. PC Barnet then handcuffed the suspect and forced him to the ground, while PC Hainault gave him another 50,000-volt charge to ensure that law and order prevailed.

1045 hrs Suspect in Asda Grove incident tries to register complaint with Desk Sergeant Willesden and claims that he is blind and that his "light sabre" was a white stick. Desk Sergeant Willesden gives him a further charge of 100,000 volts for wasting police time.

1224 hrs All officers to report to Slug and Lettuce public house in Neasden High Street to celebrate the removal from public office of a Mr Andrew Mitchell, formerly a Cabinet minister in Her Majesty's Government. Inspector Blackfriars of the Police Federation gave the toast to "a great day in the history of Britain's police service". Officers were served with an amusing new cocktail devised for the occasion, called "The Plebs' Revenge". This consisted of two parts rum, three parts whisky and four parts methylated spirits. A most enjoyable afternoon was had by all.

1800 hrs Station closed for the night due to unfortunate indisposition of all officers. Messages on station answerphone recorded various minor incidents of arson, rape, murder and terrorist activity in the borough. Sadly, there will be no time tomorrow to investigate these further, as all officers are to join five thousand strong nationwide force as part of "Operation Missed Bus", to gather evidence as to whether the late Sir James Savile should be exhumed and charged with various acts of paedophilia, necrophilia and bougainvillea.

POETRY CORNER

**In Memoriam
Andy Williams
(1927-2012)**

So. Farewell
Then
Andy Williams.

King of the
Crooners.

"Moon River"
you sang.
"I'm crossing you
In style
Some day."

And now
You are crossing
Another, wider
River.

E.J. Thribb (17½)

**In Memoriam
Valerie Eliot**

So. Farewell
Then
Valerie Eliot.

Widow of my
Fellow poet
TS.

"April is the
Cruelest month"
He wrote.

Though for
You November
Has been crueler.

Shantih, Shantih, Shantih.

Ezra J. Thribb (117½)
(Il miglior fabbro)

**In Memoriam
Dr Tom Parry Jones,
inventor of the electronic
breathalyser**

So. Farewell
Then Dr Tom Parry Jones,
Inventor of the
Breathalyser device.

"Would you just breathe
In there, sir?"

That was the
Catchphrase you
Gave to the world.

Now, alas, you
Have breathed
Your last.

E.J. Thribb (17½ units
over the limit)

YES, IT'S BORIS MANIA!

The Fab Phwoar

CAN IT be **50 years** since the lovable mop-top burst onto the scene and Britain went Boris-mad? A previously staid nation succumbed to his charms and young girls screamed his name, crying "Boris, Boris, I'm pregnant!" wherever he went. With his anti-Liverpudlian humour he made the nation laugh and filled halls wherever he went. He became the most popular act in Britain but then, at the peak of his creative powers, he sadly failed to split up with himself and continued to sing exactly the same songs as he always had.

Those songs in full ★*Love Me Do* ★*I Wanna Hold Your Wife* ★*You're Going To Lose That Job* ★*Ticket to Ride My Bike* ★*'Help! I mean Cripes!'* ★*Strawberry Blonds Forever* ★*I Am The Borus* ★*Hey Nude* ★*We All Live in a Yellow Coalition* ★*And I Love Her And Her And Her And Her* ★*Your Mother Should Know (I Can't Support You)* ...and, of course, his favourite ★*Yesterdave.* (Let it be. Ed)

DAVE ROCK SPEAKS TO THE GNOME

In part two of his interview, 70s rocker Dave Rock talks about the new chapter hastily added to his best-selling autobiography 'Lock Up Your Daughters'.

They say that if you remember the 60s you were never there. Well us old rockers have got a similar saying: "If you can remember meeting Jimmy Savile then you were nowhere near him".

When I wrote about meeting the depraved pervert Jimmy Savile, in chapters 2, 3, 4, 5 and 7-94 of my autobiography, I now realise I imagined the whole thing, due to bad shit given to me by my girlfriend. She soon came a cropper, man – headmaster caught her selling them sherbet lemons, undercutting the tuck shop, and she got expelled. So I think there's a moral in there somewhere.

But yeah, me and my band "The Gropes" did do *Jim'll Fix It* once or twice, but I knew he was a wrong 'un. Call it a rocker's sixth sense. Just the tiny contact I had with him, shaking his hand, talking to him a bit, going on holiday with him, and inviting him to be best man at my wedding, I knew I wanted nothing to do with him *(cont. p. 94)*

(cont. p. 94)

JAMES BOND: 'The 70s were a different time'

By Our Spying correspondent **Peter O. O'Bourne**

Following calls for him to resign, top secret agent James Bond has come out in defence against his disgraceful behaviour in the 70s.

"It was a different time, a world of underwater cars and khaki jackets," he said on the steps of his home, visibly shaken and stirred. "In those days, young women just threw themselves at me all the time. It seemed rude not to kill them."

"I was a completely different person then. I was Roger Moore."

ME AND MY SPOON

THIS WEEK

LORD BLACK OF CROSSHARBOUR

Lord Black, I gather you are very keen on spoons. How many millions do you have?

That is a very vulgar, bourgeois and priggish question.

In fact, people say you have to watch your spoons when Lord Black is around.

Oh, really. Nine acquittals complemented by a unanimous vacation of the four guilty spoon fraud verdicts by the Supreme Cutlery Court of the US represents a complete vindication…

But you did steal the spoons, didn't you?

Jackass. Asshole. You have no idea how the American fascistic legal system oppresses the…

Lord Black, have you just put my teaspoon in your pocket?

Repeat that misinformed allegation once more and I will be unable to resist the temptation to smash your face in.

Has anything amusing ever happened to you in connection with a spoon?

I believe it was the great American philosopher Henry David Thoreau who once memorably said of spoons that…

I'll take that as a 'no'.

© Lord Blackadder of Very Cross Harbour

NEXT WEEK: *Asil Nadir, Me and My Nadir.*

The Adventures of Mr Milibean

Fountain & Jamieson

HENRY DAVIES

NEVER TOO OLD

A new love story by Dame Sylvie Krin, author of
Heir of Sorrows and *Duchess of Hearts*

THE STORY SO FAR: Octogenarian media mogul Rupert Murdoch is relishing his moment of triumph over the hated BBC. Now read on...

AS the bright lights of Manhattan twinkled like so many falling stars far below his luxury penthouse suite in the Newscorupt building, Rupert sat in the kitchen and watched his 136" Shitachi plasma 3D TV with unalloyed pleasure.

"You gotta see this, Wend! Old Auntie Beeb is going down the dunny faster than a dingo with a firework up its doo-doo!"

However, this beautiful young bride from the land of the beansprout was in no mood to share his shameless schadenfreude.

"Time for bed, old man. It nearly 8.30."

Rupert sipped his cup of Brooks Bond PCC Tips Tea and tried to stall for time.

"Oh, come on, Wend. Just one more news bulletin about the 84-year-old perv and the young girls." Wendi eyed him curiously.

On the screen the suave figure of Adam Bulletin intoned, "First there was Leveson and Skyfall – now there is Savile and BBCfall!

Rupert cackled with delight, "Bonza banter Bulletin! Yes, it's pay-back time for Leveson. Those stuck-up BBC bastards will regret having a go at me or my name's not... What is it again, Wend?" She sighed. "In fact, I feel like tweeting!"

"No! You no tweet!" The steely voice of the martial arts expert rang through the lofty apartment.

"I told you already. No more Twitter."

Rupert's face fell and his eyes glazed over. "I don't remember that. I have no recollection of that conversation. I do not recall any exchange of that nature..."

"No! no! no! Lupert! You not at Reveson now! You lemember good. No more embarrassing tweets. You go bed, chop, chop!"

Rupert shuffled off in his Hugo-Not-Boss designer dressing-gown and slippers.

"I'm on my way to Bedford Billabong, as old Granny O'Diggery used to call it back in the big house at Bumcrack Creek..."

"You lambling, Lupert..."

Rupert opened what he thought was the kitchen door and walked straight into the huge stainless steel Zannewsi fridge.

He looked around absently. Now, what was the reason for him coming in here? His confusion was not helped by the sight of a row of mysterious Chinese rejuvenating medicines dating back to the Qwak dynasty which contained such exotic ingredients as Panda penis, Tiger's testes and genuine dragon droppings.

Jeez! He thought. No wonder his bedtime beverage tasted funny.

But then something else caught his eye. Tempting, seductive, alluring... it was his iPhoney5. What was that doing hidden in here?

"Ah, just one little tweet won't do any harm," said a devilish voice on his shoulder.

"Too bloody right," said another devilish voice on his other shoulder.

Rupert's wrinkled hand stretched out to grasp the forbidden Apple. His fingers fumbled over the "out-of-touch screen" keys, but the letters poured out of him... S.C.U.M.B.A...

"What you doing, Lupert?"

"Nothing, my little bird's nest souperwoman..."

"Come out of the flidge, at once..."

But it was too late. The message had gone winging its way across the twittersphere, through cyberspace and the digital diaspora, out into a billion handsets all over the globe – "Scumbag paedo Levenson toffs celebrity BBC perverts".

The door was flung open and there was Wendi, her eyes aflame with anger. With one deft aerial kick, she sent the phone flying out of his hand and in one balletic, yet brutal, motion she caught it and chopped the mobile handset in two, as if it were made of bamboo.

"Believe me, Wend, I haven't done anything stupid, this time. I've just made an impassioned plea for improved editorial standards and greater transparency in large media corporations."

"You having ilony bypass old man?" she shouted and slammed the door shut again with a loud clunk, plunging him into darkness. A chill ran through his veins. He was beginning to feel cold, very cold indeed...

(To be continued)

THE BBC
An Apology

WE WOULD like to apologise unreservedly to Lord McAlpine for the suggestion which we found on the internet that he was a top paedo. We now realise that this was a case of mistaken identity and was not in any way our fault, due to the fact that we were misinformed on the key issue, ie that everything on Twitter is rubbish. The top right-wing paedo that we meant to reveal is, of course, Lord Voldemort, who has a similar first name (Lord) and was therefore easily confused when we were under the pressure of deadlines and cobbling together old bollocks. Lord Voldemort is a well-known member of the establishment and although he is now dead, he spent at least ten years stalking the corridors of Hogwarts School, preying on young pupils whom he scarred for life (Harry Potter).

THE BBC
Another Apology

WE WOULD like to apologise unreservedly to Lord Voldemort for our error in identifying him as a top paedophile. We had no idea at the time that he was, in fact, entirely fictional, as indeed was our original story. *(You're all fired or rather "stepped-aside". Ed.)*

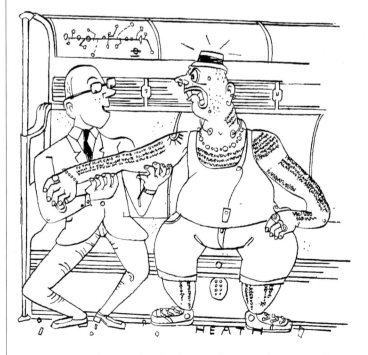

"I hope you don't mind, only I forgot to bring anything to read"

CAMERON TO LAUNCH NEW SUPER-INQUIRY INTO 'EVERYTHING'

By Our Political Staff **Justin Webbsite**

THE Prime Minister last night announced that he is to set up a comprehensive, independent, judge-led inquiry into the growing scandal of the government's reliance on setting up independent, comprehensive, judge-led inquiries into everything you could possibly think of.

"The remit of my super-inquiry," said Mr Cameron, "will be to determine whether I can continue to set up inquiries as a way of avoiding taking any action, or whether I should actually do something."

The super-inquiry is estimated to cost £2 billion and to last at least ten years before publishing its preliminary report in 2030, or long after Mr Cameron has ceased to be prime minister, whichever is sooner or later, according to the state of politics at the time.

A good way to bury bad news

The inquiry is to be headed by the late Lord Denning, who has the triple virtue of being highly respected, wholly independent and unquestionably dead.

Nob Centre

VACANCIES FOR OLD ETONIANS

CHIEF WHIP — PM — ARCH BISHOP

MP to Appear in House of Commons

There was outrage yesterday, as it was revealed that an MP was going to make an appearance in the House of Commons.

"This just demeans the world of showbiz," said one Soap Opera star in *Nuts* yesterday. "This is obviously a blatant attempt to revive a flagging career for a fast buck and a bit of free publicity."

The MP's appearance will be televised, and the edited highlights shown on seedy digital channel *BBC Parliament*.

She will be appearing alongside several minor television personalities, a few ex-estate agents, some failed local councillors, and John Redwood.

OSBORNE TRAIN-GATE ROW

Which class are you, standard or first?

Ruling, actually

"I'm going to have to let you go – you're not hitting your targets"

Han-z-z-zard

The Budget of the European Union

Rt. Hon. David Cameron *(Eton and Oxford, Con)*: I must inform the House that when I go to Brussels next week I will be taking a very tough line and insisting that they only raise the EU budget by a very modest £800 billion.

(Cries of "Hear, hear", "Shame, shame" and "What am I meant to shout now? I've forgotten...")

The Rt. Hon. Ed Ballsache *(Gord-On-Brown, Lab)*: This is a disgrace. We on this side of the House demand that this outrageous and grotesque EU budget should be frozen at 0 percent and insist that the British people would not wish us to pay a single euro more to the unelected, corrupt and wasteful Euro-dictatorship sitting there in Brussels.

(Cries of "Hear, hear, you speak for Britain" from Tory backbenchers)

Mark Foolishly-Reckless *(Rebel-on-the-Make, Con)*: That's jolly unfair, taking our lines like that. You chaps in the Labour Party are meant to be totally pro-Europe, whereas we in the Tory party are totally anti-Cameron.

(Cheers from UKIP benches)

Rt. Hon. Nick Clegg *(Pollbottom South, Lib Dem)*: This House must realise that our friends in Europe couldn't care less about what you people think and that they're going to increase their budget whether we like it or not.

The Speaker, Rt. Hon. John Bercow *(Twitter Central)*: Order, order. Mr Clegg will withdraw his remarks as being disrespectful to this House and, worse, completely true.

(General uproar as members shout abuse at each other, Mr Cameron and Mr Speaker)

Ms Nadine Dorries *(Queensland North, Monster Raving Celebrity Party)*: Can I advise the House that I shall be absent for a few weeks so that I can be on telly and be famous and earn lots of money...

(Even greater uproar, as every honourable member shouts abuse at Ms Dorries for lowering the standing of Parliament in the eyes of all right-thinking creepy crawlies)

LOUISE POT ATTACKS NADINE KETTLE

By **Kat Fight**

FORMER Tory MP Louise Pot has launched a vicious attack via Twitter on Tory MP Nadine Kettle for her decision to take part in "I'm a Celebrity Get Me Out of Here".

"Nadine doesn't care about her constituents, she just wants to be famous," tweeted Louise Pot angrily. "Next thing we know Nadine Kettle will be moving to New York and working for Rupert Murdoch."

Nadine Kettle quickly hit back at Louise Pot via Twitter,

saying, "I've not spoken to a single constituent who doesn't want to see me representing their interests by being covered in maggots whilst being force fed kangaroo testicles."

THE JOHN LENNON LETTERS
Edited by Hunter Davies

Letter 23
To the milkman, June 1958

One pint today please.

WRITTEN when John was 17, this brief note is very typically John – pithy and to the point, but with an underlying note of rich Scouse humour.

It seems likely this note was intended to indicate that John wanted just one pinta, no more, no less, delivered to the household on that particular morning.

Did John drink all the milk himself, or did he share it with his Aunt Mimi? Aunt Mimi liked a drop in her tea, by all accounts, but it is not known whether she had it at other times, such as with her breakfast cereal.

Beatle experts identify the milkman as either Richard "Dick" Trubshaw, or Ernie Smith, depending upon which of them was doing the round that day. It's a fuzzy area that continues to baffle Beatle investigators. What is known for certain is that the Trubshaw family originally came from Manchester. Dick retired from his milkround in 1966, and Smith retired from his two years earlier, in 1964, before going to live near Bangor in Wales. His informative autobiography, "I Was Lennon's Milkman" is still in print.

This legendary letter, known to Beatles academics simply as "The Milkman Letter", was sold at Sotheby's, New York in 2007 for $23,000, but would now be worth twice that amount. Professor Von Arnim, of The Beatles Institute at the University of Indiana, argues in his influential treatise "Imagine There's No Milk: John Lennon, The Milkman Letter and The Creative Muse" that this note follows an intricate mathematical formula: the first word, "one" is three letters long, the second "pint" is four letters long, the third, "today" is five letters long and the fourth and final word "please" is six letters long. Many leading Beatles mathematicians confirm the accuracy of this claim.

Today, the Milkman Letter hangs in the boardroom of the Head Office of the Chase Manhattan Bank.

AFTER the break-up of The Beatles, John wrote quite a few letters to the music press, attempting to put them right on certain details of his own musical input. Many of these letters, like this one, are alive with a rich mix of puns, spoonerisms and word-play, putting John firmly in line with other major surrealist writers and poets, like Lewis Carroll and Edward Lear.

Letter 73
To Melody Maker

Dear All, Wot a load of old crap as the actress said to the bish-up last weeks – wast leeks – article was about Revolution No. 9. Paul had SOD ALL to do with it, cos true art is not his perpendicular bag, baby. So stick that up votre arse, with loveandpeace, John and Yoko

PS: The air in our heads lifts us like birds into the sky so we can fly away on our dreams.

ONCE in New York, John and Yoko led an almost monastic life, hoping to find the simplicity which they had craved for so long. Their letters to their in-house assistants – accountant, chauffeur, two PA's, PR, cleaner, laundress, estate manager, lady's maid and valet – show how fiercely dedicated they were to a life without the pressures of fame, ambition or material possessions:

Letter 141
Domestic list for Fred, 23 May 1977

FRED
Onions
Carrots
We MUST HAVE a new car. Old car has radio tuned to WRONG channel
Matching mink coats + spares
Shoes need polishing
Peel 17 grapes to aid world peace. And make it snappy.
Complain to LAUNDERY about stain on shirt
His and her safes for jewellery, etc.
Take corn off cob
8-9000 new acres, please somewhere pleasant, maybe Vermont OR Catskills

---

FOR ten years, John and Yoko dedicated their lives to bringing peace to the world. Every now and then, they would write an Open Letter to the Planet, publishing it in the New York Times, or on a billboard on Madison Avenue:

Letter 164
Love Letter, New York Times, 27 May 1971

A Love Letter from John and Yoko To People Who Ask Us What, When And Why

When someone is angry with us, we draw a halo around his or her head in our minds. Does the person stop being angry then? Well, we don't know! We know, though, that when we draw a halo around a person, suddenly the person starts to look an angel to us. You should try it sometime! You really should! We live in a beautiful universe. Let's not spoil it with guilt. Love is all you need. JOHN AND YOKO

DESPITE the odd fall-out between mates, he continued throughout this period to send friendly missives to his old mucker, Paul:

Letter 165
To Paul and Linda McCartney, 27 May, 1971

I hope you realize what shit you laid on Yoko and me. That's not something I'll ever forgive. It makes me really fucking angry. Who the fuck do you think you are? Get off your high horses. Have you ever thought you might possibly be wrong about something?

And I wrote at least half of Eleanor Rigby so stop saying you did, jerk, so get that into your silly little perversion of a mind. Ain't you got no shame?

Power to the people.
love and peace brother
John and Yoko

The letter demonstrates the warmth of John's feeling for Paul – communicated, as always, in their inimitable Scouse banter.

Senior Beatle academics believe the mention of horses in what has come to be known as the High Horses letter is probably a reference to the $3million Wyoming stud farm Yoko had purchased the week before to add to her extensive property portfolio. "You know what?" she wrote in an Open Letter to the World in 1977, "I love the world so much, I want to possess every little bit of it".

As told to CRAIG BROWN

BBC CRISIS: DAY 94

Cameron presses Middle East leaders on human rights abuses

Can I meet the dissidents claiming to have been tortured?

They're a little tied up right now

U.S. ELECTION
An Apology

IN RECENT weeks, in common with the BBC, ITV, Channel 4 and all newspapers, we may have given the impression that the recent presidential election was developing into an unprecedented cliffhanger, with the two candidates so equally matched the result was going to be in doubt possibly for weeks to come. Headlines such as "It's too close to call", "This one's going to the wire and beyond", "Romney says Ohio's in the bag" and "Obama claims lead among swing state marginal women Latina disabled gay veterans" might have led readers to believe that Mitt Romney had some chance of ousting Barack Obama from the White House. We, of course, knew all along that there was not a jot or scintilla of truth in any of this nonsense, and that there was not a chance in a million years that such an obvious loser and charisma-free non-entity as Romney would ever get near the Oval Office. Naturally, we apologise profusely to our readers for any confusion which may have been caused by our editorial decision to publish such obvious guff, but would plead in mitigation that it was the only way in which we could attempt to drum up any interest in this otherwise tedious and interminable non-contest.

"Can you see the 'use by' date on this?"

Cameron Hails 'Middle East Winter'

The Prime Minister has hailed the "Arab Winter", which has seen fledgling political dissent across the region ruthlessly crushed by dictators using British-made arms and fighter jets.

"What a truly emotional moment it was, watching thousands of cheering British arms manufacturers pouring into the main squares in the United Arab Emirates, Saudi Arabia and Bahrain to celebrate, firing into the air as I signed multi-million pound deals to crush democracy," he said.

FOX ELECTION NEWS EXCLUSIVE

■ **America signs up for four more years of free drugs, forced abortions and mandatory homosexuality**

CHINESE ELECTION

'TOO CLOSED TO CALL'

Those Election results in full

Beijing East

There was no election. Mr Xi Jin-Ping was declared First Secretary by a majority of 0 votes. 100% swing to the Communist Party.

NEW CHINESE LEADER 'NOT AN OLD ETONIAN'

Shock Appointment Rocks World

ME AND MY SPOON

GEORGE ENTWISTLE
Director General of the BBC

Do you have a favourite spoon?

I have no idea whether I have a favourite spoon or not. No one told me what the situation was, spoonwise, and it was not appropriate for me to interfere in questions of cutlery preference.

But surely curiosity alone would make you wonder whether you had a favourite spoon?

Look, I have been extremely busy recently writing a very important speech about spoons and nobody drew any problems to my attention. I can't be expected to keep abreast of *all* the spoon-related news in the world – we live in a 24-hour, multi-platform, rolling news culture and it is impossible to know every single detail about spoons, such as whether I have a favourite one.

Don't you ever look in the drawer to see which spoons are in there?

I didn't look in the drawer on this occasion.

Isn't it your responsibility as…?

All right. I resign. I'm not up to the job. Goodbye.

Has anything amusing ever happened to you in connection with a spoon?

Yes. I'm taking 450,000 spoons with me as a pay-off for leaving.

NEXT WEEK: *Greg Dyke "Me And My Dyke".*

Daily Mail

Friday, November 30, 2012

LORD LEVESON'S LINKS TO SAVILE

AS Lord Justice Leveson prepares to issue his 'report' into the future practices of our trade, we at the Mail think it is only right to point out the huge number of worrying features he shares with tracksuited pervert Jimmy Savile.

The Mail says this not to prejudice Leveson's report, nor to cast any doubts on his recommendations that Britain's glorious, independent press should be shackled and dismembered, but because we have genuine concerns. Concerns for Britain's children. Here are those links:

● **Link 1:** A lot of Leveson's work has been transmitted on BBC news bulletins. Hated pop paedo Savile was famous for his appearances on pinko broadcaster the BBC.

● **Link 2:** Cigar-chomping deviant Savile asked people – notably the children he preyed on – how he could 'fix it' for them. Leveson has been observed repeatedly asking people what can be done to make things better.

● **Link 3:** Both men have been awarded the honour 'Knight Batchelor'. Is it really credible that they didn't meet?

● **Link 4:** Savile cultivated relationships with important politicians. Leveson has been seen inviting all sorts of senior public figures to his 'inquiry', evidently currying favour with them for his own reasons.

● **Link 5:** The name 'Lord Justice Bryan Leveson' contains the letters 'S', 'A', 'V', 'I', 'L' and 'E', as well as many more letters.

(Brilliant. More of this. P.D)

LATE NEWS

New poll shows 100% against state regulation of press

With just days before the Leveson Inquiry is due to report, an exclusive poll of newspaper editors has shown that an astonishing 100% believe there is no need for new laws or state control of the press.

"Clearly, what we can extrapolate from this poll is that there is no appetite whatsoever for tighter regulation of the press amongst a cross-section of myself," said the *Daily Mail* editor Paul Dacre.

"David Cameron must bin the Leveson Report without implementing any of its suggestions."

Said another top editor, Rupert Murdoch, "As an industry we've always listened carefully, and sometimes legally, and now it's time the Government did the same."

THE Sun SAYS

THERE can be no possible case for the draconian statutory regulation of the press proposed by Lord Leveson.

Today's press is very different indeed from that of the unfortunate period which the Leveson Inquiry has been looking into.

If his Lordship needed evidence of the huge change in attitude and behaviour of Britain's popular press, he need look no further than this editorial. Here we are, patiently waiting for him to deliver his report.

Flaw Lord

In the old days, we would have hacked his phone and bunged an official to find out the report's contents. Then we would have run a paparazzi shot of his Lordship on the toilet in his chambers with the headline "Phew Wot A Stinker!".

Then we'd have turned over his relatives, published his home phone number and urged readers to ring him up in the middle of the night to tell him that "the Law is an asshole!".

But no. Now the Sun and its sister paper, the News of the Sun on Sunday, are part of a responsible group of respectable journals of record which *(cont. until it all dies down)*

Letter to the Guardian from **DAVE SPART** *(NUJ)*

Sir,

Er... Basically... the behaviour of the British capitalist media has been totally sickening and the so-called Lord Leveson Inquiry **must** come to one conclusion and one only, ie that newspapers must be totally regulated by the state and that without strict control from reactionary central government there can be no such thing as freedom of the press…er…

Yours confusedly,
Dave Spart,

Co-chair Pro-Leveson and Anti-Badger Committee, National Union of Journalists

Letter to the Guardian from **SOME VERY IMPORTANT PEOPLE**

Dear Sir,

No one could be keener on a free press than we, the undersigned, who are all independent observers of the British media who have reluctantly come to the conclusion that there may have to be some sort of statutory regulation of the press by the government of the day in order to stop the bastards running stories about us.

Lord Trouser of Exes, Sir Jammy Dodger, Caroline Speltrouble, Zac Fishpaste, Penny Dreadful, Uncle Tom Cobblers and at least 400 others.

ELDERLY CARE SCANDAL

Gimme sheltered accommodation

New Old Rhymes

❝ There was an old woman who lived in a shoe,

She had so many children she didn't know what to do,

With the benefits cap she couldn't afford bread,

She should have had only two, as Iain Duncan Smith sensibly said. ❞

MOORE GETS CLOSER LOOK AT HEAVEN

DEVIL 'OVERJOYED' BY WOMEN BISHOP VOTE

By Our Infernal Staff **B.L. Zebub** and **Lucy Fer**

As the General Synod of the Church of England yesterday voted for the 58th time in favour of allowing women bishops, but not yet, a longtime observer of the C of E's affair said last night that this was "the result he had been praying for".

The Devil, for it was he, told reporters, "This could not be more perfect from my point of view. It makes the Church look even more ridiculous than ever, means that they will spend the next 20 years arguing about flying bishops, tearing each other apart, and entirely forgetting what they are meant to be on earth for ie discussing the importance of the living wage *(Is this right? Ed.)*"

CHURCH TELLS CAMERON 'IT'S TIME FOR WOMEN MINISTERS'

By Our Religious Staff **M.T. Pews**

PRIME MINISTER David Cameron was upbraided by the Ecclesiastical establishment, who told him they were "very disappointed" by his failure to appoint women ministers.

Said one bishop, "The Government is making itself look out of touch with the 21st Century, by steadfastly clinging on to the model of a male elite who hold all the top jobs." Said another, "How long is the Government going to talk about women ministers before it actually appoints some?

Get on with it, Mr Cameron!"

However, the Prime Minister's position is not easy, as the Women issue has caused a schism in the Cabinet, between traditionalists who don't want female ministers and evangelicals who really, really, really don't want ministers who are female.

Said David Cameron, "I hear what you're saying, but these traditions take a long time to change and until Eton accepts girls, I don't see how I can be expected to give women the top jobs."

CHURCH TIMES

Why Are There No Top Women Atheists?

ONCE again the atheist community must hang its head in shame as its upper ranks continue to be filled by men and to exclude senior female non-believers.

The headlines in the press and TV are endlessly dominated by Richard Dawkins, Philip Pullman, Stephen Hawking, Dara O'Briain, the late Christopher Hitchens... need we go on? And this raises important questions for atheism as a whole. Where are the women? Are they not allowed to say what they don't believe in? When will atheism get its act together and move into the twenty first century? Don't they realise how out of touch they *(Cont. p. 94)*

The new man believes in women bishops but not gay marriage.

What's his stance on God?

HAVE A GOOD ONE!
TAKE IT EASY
FOR YOU, MATE
SORRY YOU'RE LEAVIN'

K.J.Lamb

Nursery Times

·················· Friday, November 30, Once-upon-a-time ··················

Wicked Witch to Foster Child H. and Child G.

by Our Social Affairs Staff
Dr Foster

THE children at the heart of the current social care scandal, who cannot be named for legal reasons (Hansel and Gretel), are to be taken in by a single parent member of the Bewitching Community.

Said the local Nurseryland councillor in charge of child placement, Mary Contrary, "Look, we know she's a witch and a bit wicked and there is quite a strong possibility that she might try and put the kids in the oven, but the important thing is that she is not a member of UKIP."

She continued, "Child H. and Child G. are from Eastern Europe and it would not be appropriate for them to be fostered by anyone with views on immigration and multi-culturalism that might offend them or, more importantly, me. The wicked witch will provide a stable gingerbread home in which the children will be cooked after." *(Surely "looked after"? Ed.)*

On other pages

● *Georgie Porgie arrested on sexual harassment charge: "It was different in Once-upon-a-time," says Hairy Pudding 'n' Pie Man. "Back then you could have a kiss and a cuddle with the girls and make them cry and no one objected."* **2**

Weather latest

● *Rain, rain won't go away or come back another day* **94**

ROTHERHAM UKIP FOSTER SHOCK

Why can't the children be fostered by a group of nice Asian men?

HOW TO GET 'THE KILLING' LOOK AT HOME

1. Open your electricity bill
2. Turn off the heating
3. Put on the biggest chunky-knit jumper you own
4. Turn off the lights
5. Walk around in silence with a torch
6. Er...
7. That's it.

The Rev. J.C. Flannel (of the Diocese of Equality-on-the-Waine) **explains the situation regarding the appointment of women bishops**

YOU know there are those in the church who view the vote preventing the appointment of Women Bishops as a "real" event to be taken "literally". In this day and age, this can be seen as a somewhat outmoded view. After all, it happened so long ago (over a week, in fact) and the exact details are lost in the mists of time, that many of us in the Church of England find it hard to believe that such an amazing occurrence was an actual "historical event". Nowadays most right-thinking Bishops prefer to view the "Denial of the Women", as it is known now, as more a metaphor, a symbol of something or other, and it tells us that the Lord God is, in his vague and mysterious way, testing our credibility, and that He (or She!) wants us to use our God-given abilities to explain away this nonsense on chat shows and other televisual programmes and *(cont. Chapter 94, Verse 12)*.

BIBLICAL STORIES RETOLD FOR CHILDREN OF TODAY

David and Goliath

THIS is one of the best-loved stories in the history of the world, how the brave little hero David took on the terrifying giant Goliath.

Contrary to previous mis-tellings of this wonderful story, David was a Palestinian shepherd boy, who kept his flocks on the 24th floor of a tower block in Gaza.

The giant Goliath was the champion of the "Children of Israel".

He was a frightening figure who always dressed in heavy armour and was much feared by the poor Palestinians. They could not imagine how they would ever manage to defeat such a powerful enemy. But little David said to them all, "Don't be afraid. I have found a way to attack the giant and to bring him toppling to the ground... Just watch me."

So David strode out into the streets of Gaza armed with his homemade sling shot and five small stones.

And all the Palestinians watched him with awe.

This time, they thought, David was really going to show the Children of Israel who was boss...

So bold young David launched his missiles in the general direction of Tel Aviv in the hope that some of them might hit Goliath.

But Goliath, from under his "Iron Dome", merely swatted the little pebbles away.

He then got very angry and marched towards Gaza, assisted by several hundred aeroplanes, assault helicopters, naval warships, field artillery, heavy tanks and nuclear missiles, just in case they were needed.

And Goliath launched a fearsome attack on little David, so that he fell down dead, along with all of his family, his neighbours and nearly everyone else in Gaza.

So the moral of the story is "Don't be fooled by the Bible into thinking that you can take on Goliath, even if he has taken away all your land."

TORIES IN GAY MARRIAGE SHOCK

I won't obey

...but you will be faithful, won't you?

BRITAIN 'STILL BEING RUN BY PRIVATELY-EDUCATED ELITE' – *Shock new Sutton Trust finding*

ON OTHER PAGES

■ Bears "keep shitting in the woods"

■ Pope "still obstinately sticking to Catholic dogma"

MAN IN HOLE KEEPS DIGGING

By Our BBC Economics Correspondent **Evan Elpus**

A man who has been in a hole for several years today vowed to carry on digging his way out of the hole.

Speaking from the bottom of the hole, a hundred feet below the surface, the man, known only as "the Chancellor of the Exchequer" shouted up to baffled observers that the only way for him to get out of the hole was to maintain his so-far unsuccessful digging programme for as long as it takes.

"I'm deeper in the hole than I forecasted, but there is no doubt that I will be out of this hole far quicker the more I dig."

Some people have questioned the Chancellor's whole digging policy, asking, "Why doesn't he just stop digging and find some other way out? Possibly involving a rope – or a ladder?"

But the Chancellor dismissed these suggestions. "Ropes and ladders don't work. The only thing that works is a spade. If I keep going downwards, I am bound to reach the top. The growth of the hole shows that I am making progress. There is no Shovel B."

"I can only do this because my parents support me"

DAVID CAMERON
An Apology

IN COMMON with all other newspapers, we may in recent months have given the impression that we felt the Prime Minister, Mr David Cameron, was in some way a gutless coward who had failed to confront any serious issue with any degree of conviction and without recourse to a series of U-turns, indecision and shilly-shallying. Headlines such as 'Chicken Dave is Basket-Case', 'For He's a Jelly Bad Fellow' and 'Things Can Only Get Wetter' may have helped reinforce the idea that we had a low opinion of the Prime Minister's courage and determination. We now realise, in the light of his heroic defence of press freedom, that there is not a jot or tittle of truth in any of the above. On the contrary, the Prime Minister has shown astonishing bravery and exemplary gallantry in the face of overwhelming opposition and has proved himself the equal of Sir Winston Churchill, Henry V and James Bond (Sean Connery version) in his defence of this country's hard-won liberties. This week's headlines 'Daring Dave Defies Draconian Decree', 'Captain Courageous Takes On Liability Leveson' and 'David Cameron for Prime Minister' will, we hope, redress the balance. We would like to apologise to all our readers for any confusion arising from our previous coverage of a man of extraordinary moral fibre who is not afraid to stand up for the rights of the weak oppressed minority of hugely rich newspaper barons.

ON OTHER PAGES
● Clegg, what a pathetic loser **3** ● Miliband, another pathetic loser **4** ● The corrupt world of Mrs Clegg **5-20** ● Mrs Miliband, watch it, darling **20-93** ● Clegg kiddies, just wait till you're grown up **94**

No Prime Minister has acted this atrociously...

...since me in Love Actually

HUGH GRANT KEEPS UP PRESSURE OVER LEVESON

That Honorary Degree Citation in Full

SALUTAMUS DOMINUS BRIANUS LEVESONIUS, JUDEX FAMOSISSIMIS ET OMNIPOTENTIUS INQUISITOR INTER ETHICOS JOURNALISTICUM. SCRIPSISTI MAGNUM REPORTUM CONSISTENS DE MMMM PAGINES ET MMMMMMM VERBUM CONCLUSIONE OMNI HACKI HORRIBILE SUNT, RUPERTO MURDOCHUS SATANUS INCARNATUS, HUGHUS GRANTUS EST BONUS CHAPPUS ET CETERA ET CETERA. ERGO IMPERITIVUS EST CONSTRUCTERE MAGNAM MACHINAM REGULATORIA CUM SUBPINNINGIBUS STATUTORIAE PRO CURBERE CRIMINES JOURNALISTICENSIS ET SUPERVISIUS PER MULTOS JUDICES EMINENTES ET SAPIENS SIMILARE AD IPSUS TUUS BRIANUS CUM MULTUM ARGENTUM PER ADVOCATI PER MULTI ANNI IN FUTURUM AD NAUSEUM. *GAUDEAMUS*!

© Honorary Doctorate in Law given by Liverpool John Lennon University (formerly the Cavern Polytechnic) 2012

'TOO MANY MIGRANTS WILL PUSH UP HOUSE PRICES' says Home Secretary

By Our Political Staff **Phil Space**

The Home Secretary was condemned last night for attempting to confuse the Daily Mail. Said one spokesman, "How on earth are we meant to cope with these two conflicting pieces of emotive news in the same sentence?" He continued, "When our editor read the headline, he was furious and delighted at the same time. I thought his head was going to explode with angry joy. For a minute he stopped swearing. We were all very, very worried. It's incredibly irresponsible of Mrs May to mess with Mr Dacre's brain in this way."

ON OTHER PAGES
● Stop online porn now, says Mail Online porn service ● Stop Tax Evasion, Unless You're the Mail's proprietor, says Mail ● Editor's Head Explodes

LEVESON REPORT

Leave me alone! This is harassment!

Notes&queries

ROYAL SPECIAL

If the Duchess of Cambridge has twins, which one will become the monarch?

(Mrs Ethel Flagg-Waver)

● Under the existing British constitution, if the older twin is female and the younger twin is male, then the boy would take precedence in the line of succession to the throne. But legislation is now going through Parliament to ensure that, in such a case, the female twin, if older than her brother, would be first in line. However there is now pressure from the Lib Dems to insist that, in the case of twins being born, it would be unfair to discriminate against the supposedly younger sibling, since both have spent an identical time in utero. In this case they propose that the throne should rightly be made a "job share", with the twins ruling jointly, sitting on the throne on alternate days.

One problem with this proposal would be the question of which twin should deliver the King or Queen's speech at the opening of Parliament. This, however, could easily be solved by the construction of two thrones, side by side, from which the twin monarchs could read alternate sentences of the speech. In the case of a multiple Royal birth involving triplets, quadruplets, quintuplets or more, then a special Royal sofa could be constructed for the occasion.

Lady Candleabra Schama

Lady Candleabra is wholly mistaken in her unforgivably superficial analysis of the difficulties which might arise if the Duchess of Cambridge gives birth to two or more Royal heirs to the throne. She completely overlooks, for instance, the possibility that one or more of the children may be neither male nor female but transgender. In such circumstances, the question which will arise is whether the new TG heir to the throne should be officially titled "King" or "Queen". In my view, as a longstanding observer of gender politics as it has evolved in the British monarchical structure, it would be highly inappropriate to use either of these archaic and patriarchal terms. It is high time that a new term was devised to cover this eventuality. My own suggestion is that the honorific "Her Majesty" could be replaced by "Her Maphrodite" and Prince Andrew" by "Prince Androgyne". These, however, are merely tentative suggestions intended to stimulate further debate among your readers.

Professor Petronella Hennessy

● I'm afraid Prof. Hennessy has entirely missed the point, which is that one of the transgender twins might be a Moslem, which constitutionally would make it difficult for the putative head of the Church of England to be a woman, or a man, or indeed anything else, unless the other non-Moslem twin decided to act as Regent on the understanding that he, she or they did not embrace Buddhism, Shamanism or become a Jedi Knight, which would under current constitutional arrangements disqualify them from *(cont. p. 94)*.

"Let's see what's here? Slug, snail and ... THERE ... puppy dogs' tails, it's a boy!"

A Doctor Writes

AS A doctor I am often asked by every newspaper in the country to explain the medical condition lately affecting Her Royal Highness the Duchess of Cambridge. What happens is that a large proportion of the population become extremely sick of reading endless pages of drivel about Kate's pregnancy and end up vomiting. The doctor, in this case myself, meanwhile invoices every newspaper for £1000 and rapidly feels a great deal better. This is known in the medical profession as morning newspaper sickness, or *overhyperemesis quickbuckensis*.

© A Doctor

You name the Royal Baby

As the whole world waits for the birth of the next heir to the throne, we invite Private Eye's readers to pick a name for the royal baby that would be appropriate for the new 21st century modern monarchy.

BOY	GIRL
Boris	Diana
Mo	Rihanna
Robbie	Tulisa
Bruno	Darcey
Wayne	Posh
Evan	Nigella
Kaiser Wilhelm II	Queen Elizabeth II
Sir Peregrine	Nancy Dell'Olio

■ **Text your choice for the next King or Queen of England to 09797 943744**

Calls charged at £25 a minute. Terms and conditions apply, but we're not telling you what they are.

HOW JOURNALISM WILL LOOK POST-LEVESON

TORY FEARS

Bloody UKIP, coming over here and taking our jobs

Historic Anniversary of First Ever Text

By Our Technology Correspondent **Ivan iPhone**

IT'S EXACTLY twenty years since the first ever text was sent, changing the way we communicate forever.

It happened in the offices of Vodafone, where the engineers had been working on the technology to transmit digitised characters telephonically. One of the senior managers walked into the room and tapped out the now historic message, "Let's not pay any tax for the next twenty years ☺".

Only twenty years later texting had become so sophisticated as a means of social communication that it was being employed by the Prime Minister of the day to make himself look a complete idiot, by sending red-haired women messages such as "Hope this text doesn't get revealed in any major public inquiries, thus making me look a complete idiot. LOL *(Leveson Out Loud)*"

A Doctor Writes

AS A doctor, I am often asked by my patients, "Will these tablets do me any good?" The answer is, of course, no. The symptoms are very familiar to those of us in the medical profession. The patient sees an advertisement, is struck by an irrational craving for a tablet and then gets hold of a tablet and doesn't know what to do with it.

This is known to us doctors as the *morovirus* or *overhypemesis ipadmini kindlefire googlenexus christmus*, to give it the full technical term. Invariably, the patient ends up using the tablet only for playing stupid games like Angry Birds or watching ads on YouTube for new tablets.

This leads to further manic cravings and a vicious cycle of sickness results, with shrivelling of the brain as an obvious side-effect. There is currently no known cure for this condition but traditional wisdom claims that an Apple a day keeps the doctor away, though it should be stressed there are no peer-reviewed studies backing up this therapy.

If you're worried about overdosing on tablets, don't be, it's the only thing that's keeping the economy alive.

© A Doctor Again 2012

"I've got an amazing new app... it shows you the road ahead, so you can see where the hell you're going"

SHOCK CENSUS FINDINGS PORTRAY BRITAIN OF THE FUTURE

by Our Demographic Staff **Michael White-British**

AN extraordinary picture was revealed today of the dramatic changes which are taking place in Britain's racial, marital and religious profile.

From the 2011 Census figures it is now possible to project what Britain will look like in ten years' time.

For a start, the population of these islands will have risen to 120 million, most of whom will be living in London.

The only people who are married will be gays, as the new figures show that amongst heterosexuals, marriage has declined to only 2 percent, replaced by co-habitation, lone parenting or communal living, according to the principles of Jedi-Scientology.

Thanks to accelerated immigration and other social and demographic trends, it is clear that by 2021 the typical Briton will be a Polish Afro-Indian Muslim, whose parents were born abroad, living with a partner of different ethnic origin, who is most likely to be a Filipino-Bangladeshi-Irish-Slovak.

Only one of the couple will speak English as a first language, whilst both will rent their property jointly from a landlord who is a militant atheist.

The couple's relationship will on average last two years and 314 days.

If they have any children, 90 percent of them will have been taken into care, particularly if one or other of the co-habitees belongs to a fringe political party such as UKIP or the Conservatives.

BBC Radio 3

Opera Highlights

6pm: Berlusconi's The Marriage of Silvio

ACT ONE begins with the delighted townsfolk celebrating the downfall of the hated and despised Robber Baron, Silvio, who has been replaced by the popular and much-respected European technocrat Mario Monti-Pythone, the prime minister for silly talks.

In honour of their new German masters, the chorus switch from Italian to sing Schubert's "Vas ist Silvio?" ("Who the hell is this guy Silvio anyway?").

However, by the start of Act Two, the townsfolk have become heartily sick of the reign of austerity imposed by their new ruler Monti. He sings the haunting aria "Che manina gelida" ("Your bank account is frozen, so are your benefits, wages, pensions and everything except the prices in the shops").

The rebellious townsfolk begin to yearn for the free-spending days when the Robber Baron had handed out money to his favourite TV presenters, underage courtesans, belly dancers and prospective members of the European Parliament.

In Act Three, the people scornfully sing the classic chorus "Milione e tre" ("Who cares that the national debt is rising by a million and three euros every second?"). They demand a return to the good old days as Monti slinks humiliated off the stage and the Robber Baron reappears, announcing that he is to marry a beautiful 27-year-old local councillor. He sings the old neapolitan song "Ah Sole Mio" ("I don't know what she sees in me"). Silvio is raised shoulder-high by the delighted crowd and leads them in a final rousing rendition of the old folk dance the "Bunga-bunga".

From off stage we hear the distant sound of the Italian bond market in free fall, as Italian bankers throw themselves off the Leaning Tower of Pizza. Silvio sings "La Donna e Mobile" ("The Woman is Fickle"). *(Surely "Fifty Years Younger Than You"? Ed.)*

UNITED STATES GUN CONTROL
The Facts

1. It ain't gonna happen, buddy
2. Over my dead body
3. Correction, your dead body
4. Er...
5. That's it.

GUN

SILENCER

FRACKING 'PROBABLY SAFE' says Government

By our Energy Staff,
Eartha Quake and
Sir Tremor McDonald

THE Government today lifted its ban on shale gas exploration, using the controversial "fracking" procedure. Said Energy Secretary, Ed Davey, "Following extensive geological research, we've discovered that most of the underground black shale deposits are situated in the Midlands and the North and therefore are not at all dangerous for us. Fracking will not cause any collapses in our votes or any worrying explosions of public outrage, because the seats affected are all held by Labour." Asked whether landslides might be an issue, he replied, "Not a chance. Any seismic shift in voting patterns would have to come about by something much more catastrophic or threatening to our children's future, like gay marriage or the ordination of women bishops."

Fracking: The Plus Side

THOSE PROPOSED STRINGENT NEW AMERICAN GUN CONTROLS IN FULL

1. You are no longer allowed to buy a gun unless you have enough money to pay for it.
2. You are no longer allowed to buy a gun if you're drunk, unless the person selling you the gun is also drunk.
3. The age at which guns can be sold to kids with fake IDs is raised from 8 to 11.
4. Anyone wishing to buy a gun must prove they are able to handle the weapon sensibly by shooting the store clerk first before robbing his shop. *(That's enough. Ed)*

ALL CHANGE AT THE TIMES

Previous Editor

New Editor

Editor of Thunderer 'Forced Out'

by Our Media Correspondent **Phillippa Page**

NEWS Corp sources say the Times' editor James Harding had no choice but to resign after failing to do a terrible job, thus losing the confidence of Rupert Murdoch.

"What sort of a drongo editor is this flaming galah – he's no Rebekah Brooks, that's for sure," said Mr Murdoch.

"During Harding's five years in charge he hasn't once bought this great paper into disrepute. That means I couldn't just shut the bloody thing down and sack all these overpaid useless hacks."

"Whoever takes over this money-pit better be a lot worse at their job if they want to get an £11m payout like my flame-haired Princess Rebekah," he continued to sob.

Rupert Murdoch later tweeted this tribute to James Harding: "If he hasn't cleared his desk by two, get security to chuck him out."

LOTTERY WINNER CLAIMS RECORD PRIZE

A MIDDLE-AGED red-haired woman, who wished to remain anonymous, last night stepped forward to collect her £11 million prize from the News International Lottery. As she accepted the huge cheque from top celebrity Rupert Murdoch, Ms R.B. of Chipping Norton said, "This will not change my life. I've already stopped working, but maybe now I will move into smaller accommodation. I will, however, treat myself to a few little luxuries, like soap and snout."

D I A R Y

CELEBRATE!
My Guide
to Home
Entertaining
PIPPA
MIDDLETON

NEW YEAR'S EVE

New Year's Eve is traditionally held on December 31st. It is known as "New Year's Eve" because it comes just before New Year's Day.

The wife of Adam of "Adam and Eve" fame in the Bible was called Eve, so it's something of a birthday celebration for her, too!

Actually, I don't know anyone with a birthday on New Year's Eve – but I still take every opportunity to celebrate it!

Many people throw parties to "celebrate" New Year's Eve. The following are two of the ingredients for a great party!

i) Drink

ii) Food

Food is best served on plates, whilst drink is best served in a glass, a cup, or in some other kind of container with high sides. If your drink container does not have high sides, then the drink may spill on the floor, or down your party dress – not good news!!!

Equally, if you serve food such as "chicken drumsticks" or "beef stew" in a glass, it may be quite difficult to "get at" with a knife and fork.

At midnight on New Year's Eve, members of my family – including my sister Kate!! –always say "Happy New Year" to one another. We find it a great a way of bidding each other a "happy new year"!

PIPPA'S TIP: *I find it very helpful to take down my old calendar on New Year's Day and pin up a new one! That way you won't get your dates mixed up!!!*

VALENTINE'S DAY

It's a great idea to send your loved one a card on Valentine's Day!

You either buy a card on the high street or – even better! – make one yourself.

How to Make a Valentine's Card
What you will need:
a piece of card, a felt-tip pen.
Step One: Get someone to fold your piece of card down the middle.
Step Two: Now write a message on the inside using the felt-tip pen.

If you are throwing a Valentine's Day party, you might like to try following an old Middleton family tradition – and serve food and drink!

Be sure to serve wine or champagne. A sure-fire way to tell which is the champagne is to check and see if it sparkles or not.

PIPPA'S TIP: *When opening a bottle of champagne, be careful not to direct the cork straight at your eye or it could hurt.*

A SUMMER TEA-PARTY

Summer is the perfect season for a tea-party on the lawn or around the swimming pool.

Cucumber sandwiches are a great idea. They are very easy to make, too – you just put cucumber between two bits of bread. But do remember to slice it first, or it will be much too big to fit in your mouth.

The perfect accompaniment to afternoon tea is tea. You make tea by pouring boiling water onto a tea bag. But do be sure first to put the bag into a cup, or you could spill a lot of boiling hot water over the table, or onto your hands. If this happens, consult your family doctor at once.

Cricket and tennis are perfect summer games. They are best played outside, and are even more fun played with a ball.

PIPPA'S TIP: *Never play tennis with a cricket ball or it could hurt.*

SUNDAY LUNCH

There are no hard-and-fast rules. You can serve Sunday lunch on any day of the week. I even once served Sunday lunch on a Friday! All my friends thought it was highly eccentric or "TP" ("Typical Pippa!")

But – seriously! – it's probably best as a general rule to serve Sunday lunch on a Sunday, so that all your friends and family know exactly when to arrive!

If you and your friends are vegetarians, best not serve them meat.

As a rough rule of thumb, meat comes from animals, such as chicken (chickens) or lamb (lambs) or beef (beefs). But vegetarians prefer vegetables, particularly vegetables with little or no animal content.

Carrots lend a touch of colour to any plate. If you want to balance this with a bit of green, why not try "greens"?

I always serve Sunday lunch on a table. Without a table, people sitting in chairs have to reach down a very long way to get to their plates on the floor.

Tables are available from all good furniture shops and department stores. My sister Kate often uses them!!

For more pictures of me standing quite near a table with my famous "bottom" towards the camera, see pages 209-278.

BONFIRE NIGHT

I've always loved the sights and smells of Bonfire night. Fireworks can be great fun, particularly when lit. But do be careful not to place them in your mouth before lighting or it could hurt.

Sparklers are a special favourite. I prefer to hold them by the wiry end rather than the lit or "sparkly" end.

Why not try making it a real occasion with a real "bonfire"?

PIPPA'S TIP: *Bonfires are best made out of sticks and paper, and should always be lit outdoors. Stay well away from the flames, as they can be hot.*

Sausages are the perfect accompaniment. I always like to cook my sausages before eating them, as this makes them taste much nicer. Sausages can be eaten from either end.

CHRISTMAS DAY

In our family, we have a tradition of giving each other presents on Christmas Day.

These may be wrapped, unless they are pets, such as a dog, a cat, a new pony or a goldfish. I once tried wrapping a goldfish for my sister's present, only to find that, by the time it came for opening, the poor little thing no longer worked!

Christmas Crackers, containing a small easily disposable gift, are available from your high street or direct from Party Pieces. As a child, I used to pull them with my sister Kate! Many also contain a "paper hat" to be worn on the head, but don't wear them outside in wet or windy weather or they could get "soggy" or blow away.

As told to CRAIG BROWN

"But it was with the online community where he found true and lasting friendship..."

OBAMA WARNS SYRIA 'KILL PEOPLE PROPERLY'

By Our Middle East Correspondent **Phil Graves**

THE President of the United States has issued a stern warning to President Assad about the use of chemical weapons in the ongoing civil war in Syria.

"It is unacceptable for the Assad regime to start using gas on their own people. They've still got plenty of guns, tanks and bombs and they really should be using them to kill civilians, rather than resorting to other barbaric methods."

He continued, "There are ethical ways to murder your own population and there are unethical ways and it's very clear what the difference is. If President Assad fails to keep killing people in the approved manner, we will have no option but to send an unmanned drone from thousands of miles away and blow him up at the flick of a switch, which is the humane way we do these things in the West."

CLEGG RADIO PHONE-IN

You're useless, Nick

Thanks for calling in, Dave

Bryony Gordon

Is it me or is my column no good?

One of the great mysteries of our time is the continued success of myself. I know one is not meant to say it out loud since conventional wisdom would have us believe that Bryony Gordon is the best columnist in the world, but really? Whenever you open the Telegraph there is the ubiquitous myself, grinning at you from the front page, the features section or the op-ed comment slot.

Sorry, but try as I might I just can't find anything I write remotely interesting or amusing. All that clumsy self-deprecation, all that jolly faux-posh banter and that endless stating of the bleeding obvious about relationships between men and women! It all falls flat on its face and ends up making me feel a bit queasy. And when I deliver it in the first person, it simply makes me feel as though I am being hit over the head by myself with a sledge hammer.

So if you react like I do to Bryony and feel that you've had enough of her, I suggest you turn off your Telegraph and watch Miranda on the BBC instead.

Binge-writing over the New Year

You know what it's like – you wake up feeling terrible, wondering what you were up to the night before. And then it hits you. You were writing a column for the Daily Telegraph. The shame! The ignominy! Did I really write about Miranda? Yes, I admit it. I can't stop. It's like a disease and every year one word leads to another and before you know it you are hunched over your keyboard spewing out drivel and regurgitating other newspaper columns. Urghh!!

The sad fact is, however, that binge-writing no longer shocks anyone – it has become a way of life, particularly for me.

From The Message Boards

Members of the online community respond to the major issues of the day...

Supermarkets to stock 'ugly' vegetables

I hope the supermarkets will take this opportunity to reassess their display policy. Many veg such as turnips and carrots are "suggestive" in their appearance, as viewers of That's Life will remember only too well. Last week I was shopping with my DS (aged 4) and DD (aged 5) and we saw a man inspecting a large carrot, which he was holding at waist height. What made it worse was that his skin was rather orange, and the whole situation made me uncomfortable. I'm not sure the kids noticed, but I'm sure a lot of mums would agree that the safest solution would be to put potentially offensive veg in an "adults only" area, to avoid this kind of thing. – **Supermum**

What nonsense, Supermum! We are in our sixties and have many hobbies, including real ale, non-league football, swinging and dogging. As you can imagine, this involves plenty of good-natured banter. My husband has what some narrow-minded folk would call a "misshapen penis" (although I've seen a few funny ones in my time!). The other day I saw an unusually bulbous spring onion at the greengrocer's and I held it up and asked hubby if he'd lost something. The other customers looked puzzled, so I explained that it was a dead ringer for his you-know-what! Everyone roared at this, young and old alike, and there was no question of any embarrassment. – **Gilfy_Gracie**

Time to end the disastrous "democratic" experiment. – **Sword_of_Truth**

CALLS FOR HETEROSEXUAL MARRIAGE TO BE BANNED

by Our Social Affairs Staff

FOLLOWING a recent series of high profile marriages between straight couples, there has been renewed pressure for the goverment to outlaw "different sex marriages".

The nuptials of Mr Hugh Hefner, 86, and Ms Crystal Harris, 26, and those of Mr Ronald Wood, 65, and Ms Sally Humphreys, 34, have, critics claim, "brought the entire institution into question".

Some have described the so-called marriages as "unnatural", "abnormal" and "just plain silly" and *(cont. p.94.)*

PERSONALLY I'M BORED WITH THESE 'CHASE' SEQUENCES IN ACTION MOVIES

'WHERE'S WALLY?' FOR THE LAZY

SHE WANTS ME TO GO WITH HER TO SEE SOME BLOODY MUSICAL ABOUT THE FRENCH REVOLUTION

MISERABLE LES

LEMMINGS AGREE NOT TO JUMP OVER CLIFF – 'FOR TIME BEING'

by Our Economics Staff **Jan Lemming**

A **LARGE number of suicidal North American rodents have stepped back from the brink of catastrophe and reached an agreement not to jump over a cliff.**

The lemmings seemed to be hell-bent on charging over the cliff and plunging to their doom on the rocks below, but in a late-night, last-minute compromise deal, the leader of the lemmings secured an all-lemming agreement to delay their mass suicide until a later date.

Said one lemming, "We were all pretty keen to make the leap. We'd heard the arguments against it, but we just didn't give a damn, we're lemmings."

Another agreed, saying, "Hell, there's a cliff out there, it ain't gonna leap over itself, we should go for it." However, following a brief outbreak of sanity, the lemmings got too tired to argue any longer and decided to go home and save the jump for another day.

There was huge relief around the world and stocks and shares in everything rose sharply, except for in lemmings, obviously, because, let's face it, they're going to do it sooner or later.

"I've come up with a handy graphic to explain to the public the effect our cuts are having on the deficit"

Notes&queries

Where does the term 'fiscal cliff' come from?

● Ms Nora Virus is quite wrong to attribute this financial term to the 1963 Cliff Richard album "Cliff Goes Fiscal", which was such a hit with the gay community when it was sampled by the Pet Shop Boys in 1987. This is nonsense. Fiscal Cliff is a large natural phenomenon situated in Yogibear National Park in Wyoming and climbers have long regarded it as the ultimate challenge. More recently, thrill-seekers would climb Fiscal Cliff and then jump from the top, into Lake Doubledip below. Many of these were sophomore students from the nearby New Dworkin Institute of Economics and the term "fiscal cliff" soon became a metaphor for a self-inflicted financial crisis. I enclose a photograph of my partner and me, taken at the top of Fiscal Cliff in the Summer of 2006 (not shown).

Professor Sue Perbugge

● Professor Perbugge is, I'm afraid, sadly mistaken in her fanciful theories about Yogibear National Park. In fact, dare I say it, she's made a bit of a "boo-boo" (!). As any doctor knows, one's "fiscal cliff" (cleftus fiscalis) is a steep wall in the lower part of the intestine, leading to the Grand Union Canal via the Straits of Hormuz to the pancreas and thence downwards through the digestive tract to Fingal's Cave. This is very basic anatomy and it shows, I'm afraid, how very ignorant and out of touch this country has become, particularly when you consider how many of us, after Christmas dinner, will have felt a sharp twinge as a piece of mince pie goes "over the fiscal cliff".

Doctor Ian Fluenza, BFG, KFC, RIP

Answers, please, to the following next week:

How do you pick up a penguin?
Why does Professor Higgs have his own bo'sun?
What is Alan Yentob's real name?

DRAWING ALL FAITHS TOGETHER

Message of hope for 2013
from the **Reverend Yogi Blair**

Hi!

We all know that, whatever faith community you belong to, be it Islam, Judaism, Coptic Orthodox Catholicism, the Brotherhood of Jedward Knights or Old Mother L. Ron Hubbardism, this time of year is very special and has always been associated with charity and giving.

So what an inspiration it was for all of us across the world to see, in the UK Honours List, a more than well-deserved medal for a humble vicar's wife from the little parish of St Albion's in what my dear friend, George Dubya, the former head of the Church of the Latter-Day Morons, used to call "little old Englandland".

Yes, for many years "Mother Cheriesa", as she is known, has devoted her life, as the award put it, to "the service of women's issues" and worked tirelessly and selflessly for "charities in the UK and overseas". How wonderful that of all the women in the world who have done good works and served humanity without thought of reward, it should be Cherie whom Her Majesty the Queen has been visionary enough to single out for recognition.

I hope it is not immodest of me to think that my own little suggestion that this would be a good idea might not have fallen on entirely deaf ears! And how particularly admirable it is that those who have chosen to honour Cherie in this way should have ignored all the malicious tittle-tattle she has had to endure in recent years about her making a profit out of charitable work...

As we look for a message to live by in the new year ahead, we could not do better than to remember the motto of DAFT, that there is no such thing as a free lunch, even if it is for charity. It is certainly a principle that Cherie and I have tried to live by for many years – and I am delighted to say that, thanks to that great "Charity Organiser in the Sky", we have both been wonderfully showered with blessings, 3.6 million of them, in pounds, according to the DAFT accounts for this year alone! Bless!

Your friend, Tony

Towering figure of post-war British satire dies

by **Lunchtime O'Bituary**

For nearly five decades, William Rees-Mogg dominated the world of British satire. Scarcely a fortnight went by when the magazine *Private Eye* did not contain at least one reference to him in its pages.

He appeared under a whole galaxy of affectionate pseudonyms, from Lord Rees-Smugg and Mystic Mogg to, in the very last issue, the terrifying dragon from Tolkien's *The Hobbit*, Rees-Smaug.

Right from the earliest days of his career in the 1960s and 1970s as editor of the *Times*, Rees-Mogg provided laugh-out-loud comic material to keep Britain entertained through the dark days of the now-forgotten Harold Wilson and Edward Heath.

Mogg's Game

His legendary editorial on the imprisonment of the popular singer Sir Michael Jagger, "Breaks like a butterfly, stings like a bee", still has a starring role in every newspaper article about the Sixties ever written.

His comic catchphrases were legion, including "Time for Britain to return to the Gold Standard", "Make no mistake, the world is entering a new ice age" and "I have met 16 prime ministers and 11 presidents of the United States and only one of them had what one might consider a first-class mind".

Rees-Mogadishu

His finely honed comedy persona allowed him to play a hilarious range of roles, from an archetypal Garrick Club bore to a bumbling antiquarian bookseller.

By all those who value the need for light relief in these dark times we are living through, the incomparable figure of Lord William Rees-McGonagall, as this obscure Somerset country-gentleman-turned-renowned-ace-London-newspaperman eventually became, will be sorely missed.

Last London Smogg

Fortunately, he leaves a legacy in the shape of his equally entertaining son, Jacob Rees-Mogg, about whom his father recently wrote, "If the Conservative Party is serious about rebuilding its modernising image when Mr Cameron departs, it could do a lot worse than to select as its next leader my son Jacob, a man of the future if ever I saw one – and I speak as someone who met 18 prime ministers, 42 presidents and 17 Archbishops of Canterbury, with most of whom I had an agreeable lunch at the Garrick."

The Alternative Rocky Horror Service Book

No. 94 A solemn service for the ordination and consecration of a gay bishop

Archbishop: Dearly beloved, but only in a platonic sense, we are gathered here to annoy the traditionalists (surely "anoint the ordinand"?) and to consecrate our gay brother, but not straight sister obviously, because that would be ridiculous.

All: Ha ha ha. Indeedy do!

Archbishop: Bring forward the ordinand.

(At this point, the congregation may sing a suitable hymn, such as No. 94 "The gay though gavest, Lord, is over here")

Archbishop: Are you, N or M, a devout homosexual?

Ordinand: I am indeed.

Archbishop: But not actually *in deed*?

Ordinand: Oh no. Or only in the past anyway.

Archbishop: Do you, N or M, hereby vow to live a life of complete celibacy with your civil partner?

Ordinand: *(Winks)* Oh yes.

Archbishop: *(Taps side of nose)* Well, that's alright then. There now follows a reading from St Paul's First Twitter to the Corinthians, Chapter 13.

READING

Lay/Gay Reader *(for it is he)***:** And now abideth Faith, Hope and Chastity, these three things, but the greatest of these is Chastity.

All: Really?

(There then follows a sermon on the Mystery of the Holy Celibacy)

Archbishop: You know, in a very real sense, none of us really understands the mystical teachings of the Church in regard to the complex issues of human sexuality, but... er... er... as long as we all love each other, but not in a very real sense, very much in a non-real sense, then everything is hunky-dory rather than hanky-panky.

All: Way to go, Archbish! You tell 'em.

THE COMING OUT

(At this point the congregation shall process out of the church, possibly discussing the future of the Anglican Communion or possibly how awful the Archbishop's frock looked and how embarrassing it was that he had worn the same hat as the Dean)

© C of E Frocky Horror Service Book, 2013.

SNOWMAGGEDON BRINGS CHAOS AND DESTRUCTION

*by Our Weather Staff **Peter Snow**, **Dan Snow** and **David Frost***

THE Snowmaggedon storm widely predicted to kill thousands and plunge Britain back into a new Ice Age hit the UK with full force yesterday.

Much of Britain woke to a nightmare of nightmarish proportions with as much as a few centimetres of snow falling in much of the country, with many drivers getting their gloves wet wiping a bit of slush off their windscreens, and weeping children preparing for the horror of having to go to school "like every other day".

Many drivers simply abandoned their cars in car parks after they'd finished their journeys, only returning to them after they'd finished work.

Meteorologists said Britain had never seen snow like it before, apart from Scotland every other week, and that doesn't count.

Despite the worst seeming to be over, people were warned not to leave their houses unless they wanted to.

Daily Mail
FRIDAY, JANUARY 25, 2013

NEW IMMIGRATION SHOCK

*by Our Immigration Correspondent **Michael Whiteout***

THERE was barely repressed hysteria from Conservative backbenchers, UKIP and Migration Watch yesterday, as seemingly overnight, the UK was suddenly flooded with pasty-faced smiling immigrants from abroad.

The immigrants, widely rumoured to have swept in from the continent, were suddenly everywhere, filling nice towns and villages up and down the country.

"They're in our parks, in our gardens, out on the streets," said one angry MP. "They're loitering outside at the moment, but I'm sure it will only be a matter of time before they all start applying for housing."

"A lot of them have carrots," agreed another. "It just goes to show, if you dangle a carrot in front of these types, they'll take it."

The spokesman for the immigrants, Mr Frosty D. Snowman, assured the country that they were merely seasonal workers, and come the summer they'd be long gone.

An assurance that this paper finds hard to believe.

Advertisement

Met Office

Weather information
What is snow?

For those of the population of Britain who have never experienced this strange phenomena before:

Snow is atmospheric water vapour (or 'rain') frozen into ice crystals and falling in light white flakes or lying on the ground as a white layer.

"No, Oates! Not with your scarf tied like that! It makes you look continental"

LATE (*Ok, Cancelled*) NEWS

● Should Heathrow have a first runway? Plans to open a runway at this major airport have been ruled out again on the grounds that it is impractical to have one runway actually functioning during peak periods.

QI* Facts

Britons have 50 different words for snow. Whenever it starts snowing you will hear them use one of the following words:

F*!**

Sh*!**

B*****!**

A*!**
(That's enough words. Ed.)

✥ Quite Innuit.

RAILWAY TIMES
FRIDAY 24 JANUARY 1829

Protests Grow Over Mr Stephenson's 'Rocket'

by Our Man in Liverpool, and much later in Manchester, CHRISTIAN WOLMAR

THERE were angry scenes today as passengers on Mr Stephenson's ingenious new transport device objected to the name "The Rocket".

Said one, "We thought it referred to the speed of the locomotive and not to the fare structure."

Said another, "The ticket price went up every hour we were on board. It's a rip-off by the privatised rail company which has a monopoly."

Mr Stephenson defended his "Rocketing Fare" invention, saying, "Why do you think it's called the Gravy Train?"

When challenged by protesters, the Minister for Railways, Mr Simon Burns-Money, said:

"I wouldn't know. I travel by horsedrawn carriage, so that I can read my red boxes without being disturbed by angry passengers."

Pseudo MUSICAL Names Pseudo Names

...While in the waiting room of the gender reassignment clinic my friend and I were reading Letters (1322) and we noticed that the Lookalike of Ian Hislop and Doris Day (Not funny or clever, by the way. Ed.) that we presume was sent in by our good friend Eva Will B. Will Be was assigned to an Ena Will B. Will Be. Knowing Eva, she will be too shy to point this out but I think the record should be put straight.

> K. (SARAH) SERRER,
> WATT (HEATHER) WILBEY-
> WILLOUGHBY.

...My local Sainsbury's already has an aisle for Christmas items, which seems a premature harbinger of the festive season. Here in Sweden we eschew such opportunism.

> SVEN DEREDREDROBEN.

...We do hope that when Mr Gove's new baccalaureate is introduced, it will include William Blake's beautiful poem.

> ANDY DOESFEAT,
> IAN H. CHENTIYMES.

Greetings from South America! My British-born secretary is missing her many friends and relations at home at this time of year, so may I join her in wishing each and every one the compliments of the season.

> JAVIER ZELFA
> MARY LIDDLE-CRISS (MISS).

...Howdy pardners! Reckon there ain't no finer way of passing the quiet times on a cattle drive than reading Pseudo Names round the campfire, sent in on cards and letters by nice folks I don't even know.

> RYAN STONE (COWBOY).

...The recent resurgence of the Rolling Stones has led to relentless teasing of me. Had my Scottish father and Libyan mother realised, they may have considered a different name.

> A.A.U.U. GADDAFI-MCLEOD.

...I shot the sheriff.

> BOB, Mali.

...I didn't shoot the deputy!

> ERIC, Clacton.

...It is quite understandable that your correspondent Mr Gaddafi-MacLeod blames his parents for the ridicule he has had to endure. In my own case, Tom Jones is to blame.

> Y.Y.Y. de LYLER.

...We are pleased to announce the formation of the first Rod Stewart fan club in mainland China.

> HUEE AH
> SEI LING.

...I bumped into Gerry Marsden over here in Germany the other day and embarrassingly I couldn't remember any of his songs.

> YUL NETHER-WAUGH (Cologne).

...Prior to meeting your correspondent Ms Gaddafi-McLeod, I had assumed I was alone in being teased for having a name reminiscent of a Sixties pop song, but then I saw her face.

> IRMA B. LEVER.

...How sad to learn that Irma B. Lever (Pseudo Names, Eye 1337) has been teased because of her name. Perhaps she would find it helpful to join a group?

> A.A. WEIR, D. MONKEASE.

...I sympathise wholly with your correspondent Yul Nether-Waugh (Cologne) who failed to recall the names of any Gerry and the Pacemakers songs upon bumping into Mr Marsden. We suffered a similar embarrassment when we met Ray and Dave Davies in the supermarket recently.

> AL DAY and OLIVER NIGHT,
> WALTER TOU SUNSETT,
> SONNY AFTERNOON.

...In view of the ongoing financial meltdown, what are the chances of the Rolling Stones becoming homeless?

> JIMMY SCHELTA.

...Please can you confirm that the Beach Boys were not harmed by the tidal wave shown in "Forgotten Moments in Music History" (Eye 1338), as there is much concern for their safety in the Anglo-Chinese community here in South Africa.

> SIR FINN YU (S.A.)

...In Spain, we are very fond of your British boy bands and we hope that Harry Styles et al come on an Iberian tour.

> JUAN DIRECCIÓN.

...It's not helpful to suggest that Irma B. Lever should join a group (Pseudo Names, Eye 1338). I recommend travel.

> LARS TRAYNTOR-CLARKE (Seville).

...We now understand why some of your readers have been dumbstruck when meeting famous musicians. We recently met Benny Andersson and Björn Ulvaeus at our local car boot sale and could not remember the name of a single Abba song.

> NOREEN MEE,
> NOREEN EWE.

...Should anyone doubt the veracity of your two correspondents who couldn't remember any Abba songs (Noreen Mee, Noreen Ewe – Pseudo Names, Eye 1340), I can provide first-hand corroboration of their story; I was right behind them.

> R. HARR.

...Unfortunately, Noreen Mee and Noreen Ewe have reopened an old wound for me (Pseudo Names, Eye 1340). I have never forgiven my Anglo-Greek parents for being obsessive Abba fans.

> TAKI CHANSON-MEE.

...How can Noreen Mee and Noreen Ewe not recall a single Abba song? We are surely not alone in being extremely grateful for every one of their fantastic hits.

> FRANK YEW
> FORD DE MUSSIK.

...All us girls in the Royal Horse Artillery just love Abba.

> SUE PARR (Trooper).

...I believe that being unable to remember a single Abba song was instrumental in exacerbating my dyslexia.

> WALTER OO.

...We're off to Syria to sing "I got you, babe" to President Assad, with a view to helping the peace process.

> SUNNI AND SHIA.

...We are horrified at all these ABBA fans who can't remember any of their songs. Such a great band with a profound impact on the music scene. It takes just a few bars of one of their intros and we're off, although admittedly age dims the memory on some of the lyrics.

> DEE WINNER
> JAKE C. HALL.

...Whilst it has been good to hear that there are some ABBA fans out there, you might want to know that Bruce Springsteen has a very loyal following amongst Swedish expatriates like myself.

> BJORN INTHER (USA).

...I am holding a party on Saturday night with the intention of remembering Abba lyrics. I would very much like to invite your three correspondents from Eyes 1340 and 1341 – Noreen Mee, Noreen Ewe, R. Harr.

> TERRY SNUFFING (Weekend do).

Forgotten Moments In Music History

Of course, the vibrations weren't always good

The neighbours thought Mr Suggs Snr must work in the planning department

Young Elton's spelling was mostly good

HMG TO GO INTO ADMINISTRATION

by Our Financial Staff **Robert Pest** and **Stephanie Flounders**

THE political and business worlds were shocked last night by the news that one of the most famous and long-established institutions in Britain was on the verge of bankruptcy.

Receivers were called in to take over the affairs of HMG, which, as everyone knows, stands for Her Majesty's Government.

It has been obvious to market analysts for some time that HMG was heading for very serious trouble, as year after year it racked up ever-growing debts and was forced to borrow tens of billions of pounds to stay afloat.

HMG goes pop

Worse, it became increasingly clear that its management team, headed by CEO Dave Cameron, had no strategy for reducing HMG's debt burden.

Said one analyst, "They just kept on assuring the public that they were reducing their debts, when it was quite obvious that this was entirely untrue."

Plan B-side

Said another, "Cameron and his number two, George Osborne, simply told everyone that the market would pick up and that the High Street would recover – but this was just wishful thinking."

The collapse of HMG will inevitably trigger a massive crisis throughout the country, resulting in the loss of millions of jobs.

However, insiders were last night confident that Britain could weather the storm.

"We simply don't need HMG any more," said one. "That's not how the world works in the 21st century, when everything is done via the internet.

"So long as we've got Amazon, Google, Facebook and Apple, then who needs people like Cameron and Osborne? They are soooo yesterday – as, indeed, is the whole idea of HMG."

The Many Faces Of Andy Murray

| Defeat | Disappointment | Frustration | Triumph |

"I meant to warn you about our new hand dryers"

Cluff

Fury Over Queen's Portrait

by Our Woman On The Spot HILARY MANTEL

There were angry scenes at Hampton Court, when a new royal portrait was unveiled. The picture of Anne of Cleves, by top modern artist Hans Holbein, was greeted by gasps of disbelief. "It looks nothing like her," shouted one angry king (Henry VIII). He continued, "I don't know much about art, but I know what I don't like and that's her."

Holbein's ultra unrealistic style has got him into trouble as he presented the future queen in a deeply flattering light. "He's made her look far too young and attractive. Where are the bags under her eyes? Where's the five o'clock shadow?" demanded royalist, writer and saint, Sir Charles More, writing here in the Daily Tudorgraph. But the royal sitter was delighted. "I think Hans has done a marvellous job. He's painted my head just where I want it – on my shoulders. What more could a future queen want?"

On other pages

'Heretics free to wear crosses as they burn,' promises King Henry 3
Horsemeat found in pigeon found in pheasant found in swan – feast cancelled 4
Top minstrel David Bowie releases new song 'Greensleeves', about his time in Boleyn 94

The Secret DIARY OF DAVID CAMERON aged 46¼

Monday

I was not inconsiderably incandescent this morning to discover that I haved turned into my predecessor. When I shared this thought with my wife Sam over our breakfast of Farage's Fruitcake Loopies, she said, "Are you referring to Mrs Thatcher?"

"No," I told her. "Once again, you have missed the point. The prime minister into whom I have turned, in my judgment, is Mr John Major."

I explained to Sam that when Mr Major was prime minister he had been forced to spend his entire time arguing about Europe with some fellow Tory MPs whom he rightly called "Bastards".

"Almost every night," I told Sam, who appeared to be suffering from lack of sleep due to her constant yawning, "poor Mr Major had to spend hours writing the names of these in no small measure Eurosceptic traitors in a special book he had purchased from Ryman's entitled 'My Bastards Book'."

"You're not a bit like Major," said Sam, waking up with a smile on her face. "The only *curry* you fancy is the one you offer to Tory donors if they fork out more than £50,000!"

Once again, she had, to my mind, totally missed the point. Oh, yes.

● **Tomorrow**: *How I relaunched John's historic Traffic Cone Hotline initiative and told Mrs Frau Merkel why I couldn't give 100 percent backing to her plan for total political integration of the EU at this moment in time. Oh, no.*

Nursery Times

Friday, January 25, 2013

HORSE FOUND IN FOOD CHAIN

by Our Medical Staff **Dr Foster**

TRACES of horse were yesterday discovered in an old woman.

The old woman had been assured that eating a horse would not harm her and that people on the continent ate horse all the time with no ill effects.

The horse suppliers had, moreover, sold her the horse originally in order to catch a cow which she had eaten earlier to catch a goat, to catch a dog, to catch a cat, to catch a bird, to catch a spider, to catch a fly.

Said one doctor, "There are reasons why horse is not part of a recommended diet and, though tragic, it is not surprising that the old woman who originally swallowed a harmless fly ended up as a horse-related fatality."

● *Dopey banned for life from mining after tearful confession*
● *Banbury Cross banned as unacceptable religious symbol*
● *Snowman's flight to North Pole cancelled due to bad weather*

President calls for ban on 'military-style weapons'

by Our U.S. Staff **A.K. Fortyseven**

The President of the United States, Mr Barack Obama, today indicated his determination to make a renewed stand against the availability of advanced weapons, which he said "in the wrong hands, can lead to the death of innocents".

He was referring in particular to a weapon known as "the drone", which can fly over remote areas and then drop suddenly out of the sky on top of villages, schools, and wedding parties. "It is time we stood up to the weapons lobby and refused to buy any more of their drones, which have been freely available to trigger-happy Americans for far too long."

He continued, "Hang on, what am I saying? Er... can I reconcile these two seemingly contradictory positions? Yes I can!" *(Reuters)*

Supermarket Rasen

4.00 ▶ **The Tesco Profit Chase**

Those runners in full

2-1 favourite	**Findus Boy**
4-1	**Lasagne Lad**
200-8	**Black Butey**
7-1	**Bolognese Saucy Ned**
50-1	**Rum Red Meat**
Not running	**Genuine Beef**

The Eye's Controversial New Columnist

The columnist who's got his thumb firmly in his cheek

This week I am *extremely* angry about the removal of child benefit from higher income families! Granted, my family does not need the money, as I earn a great deal from my leading newspaper column, but, as with all these things, it is the *principle* which counts! This is why I have organised all like-minded babies in my nursery into a day of action. Tomorrow, at a given signal, we will all lie on the floor and do nothing, and *(cont. p. 94)*

ARMSTRONG SHOCK

How many times a week did you take drugs?

"It's such a shame, Lance Armstrong has stigmatised us all"

An open letter from the Rt Hon David Cameron, Prime Minister of Great Britain to the peoples of Romania and Bulgaria

Dear Romanian and Bulgarian persons,

I know that all 29 million of you are thinking of moving to Britain at the end of this year, when you are allowed to do so under the rules of the EU (of which Britain is still a member at the time of writing).

However, I feel it is my duty to warn you that this would be a terrible idea.

You may have been told that Britain is a rich, successful, happy and very generous country, that is only too willing to welcome immigrants to its shores where they can live a full and rewarding new life with full access to a wide range of state benefits.

But I'm afraid this is a completely misleading picture. What is very important for all 29 million of you to realise is that Britain is in fact a disaster area, where no one in their right mind would want to live, let alone move from somewhere as lovely as Bulgaria or Romania.

Here are my top 10 facts about Britain which you should know and which should persuade you that it would be particularly idiotic of you to want to come here.

1 Britain's economy is on the verge of collapse, with a national debt larger than that of Greece.

2 Britain's government is having to borrow billions of pounds every day just to pay off the interest on the record sums it has already had to borrow.

3 Because Britain was not sensible enough to join the euro, we can't even get a bailout from Germany (which, incidentally, is a very beautiful country with a thriving economy and lots of job vacancies just waiting to be snapped up by people like yourselves).

4 Britain's once beautiful countryside is being destroyed by high-speed trains, wind farms and the building of millions of new homes which have already been allocated to immigrants from Poland (a beautiful country, by the way, which has millions of jobs left vacant by people who have gone to Britain and which could be yours).

5 Britain has the worst weather in the world. It rains all the time from January to December and large parts of it are permanently flooded.

6 When it isn't raining in Britain, it is snowing and all its roads, railways, airports and schools are shut. Other countries in the EU cope much better with this kind of thing than Britain, such as Lapland, which, as it happens, has a great many vacancies for reindeer, herders and assistants to Father Christmas, which are just waiting to be filled.

7 If you have children, they will almost certainly be confiscated by Britain's notorious social workers and put into care homes to be abused by popular entertainers from Britain's television industry.

8 If you fall ill in Britain, you will be put in one of the National Health Service's notorious hospitals, where you are very likely to contract a superbug infection and die alone on a trolley in a corridor which has not been cleaned for three weeks, owing to the outsourcing of all such services to private contractors under PFI contracts by the last Labour government.

9 This is not to say that Britain's current government is any better, thanks to the fact that it is now run by a shambolic coalition which cannot agree about anything and, therefore, does nothing as the country falls apart and turns into Europe's answer to North Korea (which, incidentally, is a charming country with many job vacancies, owing to the fact that everyone is either locked up in prison or starving to death).

10 Britain has declined into such a desperate state, thanks to its hopelessly dysfunctional and incompetent government, that its people have been reduced to eating horses, something which would never happen in a civilised country such as Romania or Bulgaria (which you may not know are beautiful, happy, prosperous countries where people should be sensible enough to stay put and not get any ludicrous ideas about emigrating to a Third World dump like Britain).

Yours, hoping not to see you soon,

David Cameron

THE BODY IN THE SUPERMARKET CAR PARK

The crucial evidence that proves it's Richard III

by Our Archaelogical Staff **Gloria Summer**

1. The body was found in a disabled space.
2. Near a hump.
3. And a 'Yorkie' bar wrapper.
4. During a winter of discontent.
5. DNA reveals remains of Richard's horse nearby, in aisle seven.

Keith Richard III

Anglo Saxon Chronicle
1 February 683 AD

Islamicist Takeover of North Africa poses threat to Europe

by Our Man in Timbuktu **Prester John Simpson**

THE KINGDOMS of Christian Europe last week vowed to unite in taking serious action to halt the spread of extremist militants calling themselves "Muslims" across the deserted wastes of Northern Africa.

In recent years, these murderous fanatics have emerged from their remote strongholds in Arabia, to take over one country after another in an unstoppable march towards world domination.

Last night, the leader of the Franks, François the First (known as "The Pathetic"), pledged to send an army of Frankish warriors to "throw back the Islamicist hordes from the very gates of Christendom".

He was soon supported by the chieftain of the Anglo-Saxons, David the Unready, who announced that he would be showing solidarity with his Frankish ally by sending 300 highly-trained British fighting men, on condition that they didn't do any fighting.

"This war for the future of European civilisation could last for decades," he warned. "I can foresee this struggle continuing as far into the future as the 21st Century."

"I'm collecting for Syria"

POETRY CORNER

In Memoriam
Andre Cassagnes, inventor

So. Farewell
Then
Andre Cassagnes.

Inventor of
The Etch-a-Sketch,
Top-selling toy
Of the 1960s.

Yes, we all
Remember turning
The knobs
To draw
A line on
The screen.

Now, sadly for
You, it is the
End of the line.

The picture has
Been shaken
And all is
Blank.

    E.J. Thribb (17½)

In Memoriam
Mick McManus

So. Farewell
Then
Mick McManus.

You were a star from
The Seventies.

You liked wrestling,
But only with people
Your own age.

    E.J. Thribb (17½ stone)

In Memoriam
Keith Campbell, Biologist
(1954-2012)

So. Farewell
Then
Keith Campbell.

You were
The scientist who
Worked on cloning
Dolly the Sheep.

We shall not
See your like
Again.

Then again,
Perhaps we will
In due course.

    E.J. Thribb (17½)

FIRST DRAFTS

Naomi Wolf 'Vagina – A New Biography'

Rupert Everett

One Direction 'Forever Young' The Autobiography

Oliver Sachs 'Hallucinations'

In Memoriam
Dave Brubeck,
1920-2012

So, Farewell
Then
Dave Brubeck
Composer, Pianist and
Jazz Legend.

Take Five
Yes, that was your hit song.

A clever pun on complex
Time signatures
And having a short break.

Now you are having
A longer one.

All together now
Doo-do-dedo-do do do
Doo-do-dedo-do do do
Dooby do do, dooby do do
Etc etc.

    E.J. Thribb (17/18)

If you'd like to hear that song again,
tune in to any documentary on BBC2
and it'll be playing over the credits,
as Alan Yentob's name appears for
some reason.

Blair at Sixty

So. Tony Blair,
You are sixty.

We would sing
"For he's a jolly
Good fellow."

Only you aren't.

And then someone
Should shout "speech!"
Except we can't
afford your fee.

Would you like
A present?

Too bad – all you've got is
The past.

    E.J Thribb (17 years,
    6 months and 45 minutes)

In Memoriam
Eddie Braben

So. Farewell
Then Eddie Braben,

Unsung scriptwriter
Who turned
Morecambe and
Wise into
Household names.

This is a
Eulogy wot
I wrote.

    E.J. Thribb
    (17½ million viewers)

"I wish you'd go back to reading a real newspaper at breakfast then I wouldn't have to see your face!"

HEATH

HELICOPTER GUNNER PRINCE HARRY ADMITS 'YES, I'VE DOWNED A FEW'

by Our Military Staff, **Major Gaffe** and **General Embarrassment**

IN HIS frankest interview yet, Prince Harry has gone into the detail of his night-time sorties with the army, which have resulted in "a large number of dead bottles".

The prince said to reporters, "Where am I? Oh yes, look, I'll be honest, there were several incidents involving a lot of shots and some people got slaughtered, including me."

He continued, "My army training has prepared me for the job in hand, ie to take a lot of drinks out of the game, which is usually strip billiards." When asked if he hated the enemy, he said, "Yes, there are some bad journalists out there and if they're targeting me, I'll try and leave the club out the back."

At that point the interview dramatically ended, as the bell went and Harry and his crew scrambled to the bar to pick up their orders.

On other pages

'I'VE KILLED' ADMITS PRINCE CHARLES

IN a highly dull TV interview Prince Charles has admitted that since starting his tour of duty as King-in-waiting he's killed a lot of time – over 60 years, in fact, and it never gets any easier, even *(cont. p. 94)*

From The Message Boards

Members of the online community respond to the major issues of the day...

Sexual services at care home

Guys, I couldn't help but smile at the story about the care home in Eastbourne booking a stripper and call girls to "sexually enable" the disabled residents. The stripper's details came from good old Tuppy Owens who was the lady behind the Sex Maniac's Diary, which yours truly used to get in his stocking every Christmas! (Although I see the Tupster went on to do the Safer Sex Maniac's Diary, which doesn't sound half as much fun.) – *Bogbrush*

As a Reader in Sexual Cultures, may I point out that this is not a question of "fun". Tuppy Owens is a respected sex therapist, founder of the Sexual Health and Disability Alliance, and the first person to publicly demonstrate the correct way to put on a condom. And safe sex is not the only consideration. Both parties should be counseled, to ensure that the person with the disability has a meaningful and fulfilling experience spiritually and emotionally and that the sex professional is comfortable with her career choice and is also fulfilled. These stories do NOT always have a happy ending. – *Dr_Sarah_Reeves*

that's cos happy ending's cost extra 🙂 – *hatfied_gooner*

As a patriot, I was delighted to see that Solitaire, the stripper in question, is a 34D. Slightly under the British average (34DD) but comfortably above France, Germany and Italy (all B). You don't get many of those to the pound! (Or the euro!) – *Thanks_for_the_mammaries*

in eastborn solitares the only game in town lol! – *Danny_Daz*

I read that when a "client" is being "serviced" by one of these "sex workers", the staff place a red sock on the door handle as a sort of "do not disturb" sign. Am I alone in finding this unspeakably vulgar? Red socks should remain the province of Baron Grade and American baseball teams, neither of whom has a place in any self-respecting institution. – *Hugo*

Hope old Tuppy showed them how to put the sock on the handle safely. – *PC_Gonmad_Elf'n'Safety_Division*

My husband and I are in our sixties and have many hobbies, including real ale, non-league football, swinging and dogging, and we've been to some terrific disabled nights at care homes throughout the Midlands area. Their aim can sometimes be a bit hit and miss but as my hubby says, any hole's a goal! – *Gilfy_Gracie*

Speaking with my PR hat on, I'm loving this feel-good story! The GB Paralympians led the way, and these guys are showing some serious British spunk! – *Hattie*

not bein funny but it say's they checkd all the prostute's 4 diseas but how do u catch disibility? – *Hayley_321*

 Dave Snooty AND HIS NEW PALS

HEIR OF SORROWS

by Dame Sylvie Krin, author of *Duchess of Hearts* & *You're Never Too Old*

THE STORY SO FAR: Charles is relaxing after a hard day's work firing off letters to government ministers about paper wastage in government ministries. Now read on...

CHARLES lay back in the free-standing, Victorian roll-top bath with its original brass lion's feet made in the Birmingham foundry of Messrs Enfield and Whitehouse in 1852. He soaked up the essential unguents of the Duchy Original Oatmeal and Tweed Bath Balm and toyed with the miniature off-shore windfarm floating happily in the foamy water.

This really is, well… not appalling at all, he thought to himself… but something was missing. Of course, some soothing music! He rang a small bell and the figure of Sir Alan Fitztightly shimmered into view through the steam.

"Beetroot yoghurt shampoo, sire?" he enquired. "No, no, Sir Alan. I was wondering if you'd be so good as to turn on the new-fangled wireless thingy."

The white begloved hand of Fitztightly activated the Andrew Roberts Radio, a gift from Charles' grateful tenants in Poundland and the radio burst into life.

"It's Radio Three, sire," said Fitztightly over the haunting strains of the National Tibetan Horn and Windchime Ensemble.

"And remember, sire, don't fiddle with the knob," Fitztightly winked. "As we used to say to dear old Backstairs Billy in Clarence House."

Charles frowned at this vulgarity as Fitztightly left the room, walking backwards and bowing. But no, this music wasn't what he wanted at all. Why couldn't they play something agreeable like one of Sir William Parry's Anthems. How did that one go…? I was glad when dum-di-dum-dum, or was that the other one?

Charles' moist hand leant over to the controls of the digital device. Blow Fitztightly – he was his own man, after all. If he wanted to change station, he jolly well would. After a moment of crackle, the inimitable tones of Radio 4's Ed Stilton boomed out.

"…and so the Queen has decided to abdicate in order to make way for the next generation."

Charles leapt out of the bath in unbridled excitement, sinking the off-shore windfarm, showering the marbled floor with soapy suds and knocking the radio into the bath with a bang and a fizz. But he barely noticed. "This is incredible," he shouted. "Why wasn't I told? The moment I've been waiting for my whole life has arrived."

He grabbed one of the two white fluffy monogrammed towels marked "Ones" and "Hers", tied it around his waist and raced out of the room and down the stairs.

"Cazza! Cazza! Have you heard the news? Mater's finally done the decent thingy!"

HE BURST into the Mountbatten drawing room where his beloved wife Camilla was sitting on the Louis Walsh XV sofa, reading the Daily Mail and hastily stubbing out an untipped full strength Old Navy Shag cigarette.

"What's the matter, Chazza?" Camilla looked up at the half-naked figure of her husband in amazement.

"You look like one of those native dancers we saw in the Gilbert and George Islands."

But Charles could hardly contain himself.

"I just heard it on the radio. Unbelievable news! The old girl is shuffling off the throne!"

Camilla pointed at page 9 of her newspaper. "Yah! I saw that! Queen Beatrice of the Netherlands to abdicate. Didn't I sit next to her at that ghastly dinner with all the dictators at Buck Pal? You know, the one for the King of Abu Dhaba Doo?"

Panic-stricken, Charles grabbed the paper and devoured the small news item beneath a large photograph of Clare Balding and her civil partner: "Dutch Queen Hands Over to Grateful Son – Amsterdam House Prices Soar."

The royal blood drained from Charles' crestfallen face and the shower cap on his weary head felt even more like a mockery of the Crown.

Upstairs he could hear the bathwater gurgling down the drain, like so many hopes and dreams…

(To be continued.)

Clegg's son 'to go to St Cakes'

by Our Education Staff
Hugh Turner

THE Deputy Prime Minister, Nick Clegg, last night claimed that he and his wife were perfectly entitled to put down their son for the exclusive, £70,000-a-term Midlands independent school St Cakes (motto *"Quis paget entrat"*).

Mr Clegg issued a statement pointing out that it was his son's "basic human right" to enjoy a proper education of the kind he himself had enjoyed, and which was sadly not available in the state educational system.

"As a Lib Dem," he continued, "I of course believe that people should not be able to buy a better education for their children, and that the public schools are a corrosive influence on Britain and a hindrance to social mobility.

"However," he went on, "if I am forced to make a choice between my firmly held principles and the interests of my children, then it is the children who must always come first – mine obviously, not yours.

"Anyway," he concluded, "in the end, this was my wife's decision. Marriage is a lot like the Coalition – I spend hours agonising over my priniciples and then I'm told what I am going to do."

MY NAME'S DOWN FOR ETON

MY NAME'S DOWN FOR ELTON

TORY BACKBENCH REBELS DENY GAY RUMOURS

Y.M.C.A*

Go ♫ Westminster

In the Tory ♫

(*Young Men's Conservative Association)

The trail of terror that reaches all the way from an Albanian abattoir to the food on your plate

by Our Entire Investigative Staff **Donna Kebab** and **Joshua Frozenburger**

A Private Eye investigation covering 37 countries across the world has revealed an extraordinary network of criminal fraud extending through every corner of the now globalised meat industry and stretching right up into the heart of government.

On 23 November last year, a 25-kilo box of frozen horse meat left a tiny slaughterhouse just outside Enverhoxhagrad in the mountains of Albania on a Polish-owned 10-tonne truck bound for the Gloupe processing plant in Luxembourg, owned by a Franco-Mexican consortium registered in Liechtenstein.

By late on the afternoon of 27 November the same consignment had been relabelled as Top Quality Pig Meat and was on its way via a 20-tonne truck to a packing plant in Denmark owned by Onag, a Finnish-Irish multinational based in the Cayman Islands.

Yet only four days later, on 31 November, this same consignment of "pork" had been mysteriously reclassified as "Poultry Meat" and was being transported in a refrigerated 30-tonne to a packing factory in southern Spain where it was parcelled up into low-end supermarket meals like "Czech Chicken in a Basket".

From Andalucia, it was only a short sea journey via Cyprus and Montenegro to Britain's leading container port in Felixstowe, from where the horse-turned-pork-turned-chicken was carried by a fleet of 40-tonne lorries into the freezer cabinet of local UK supermarkets, now yet again relabelled as "Finest Ocean Tuna Burgers", from where it was fed yesterday to innocent kiddies in local schools and unwitting old folk in care homes, millions of whom might well die immediately *(Is this right? Ed.)*

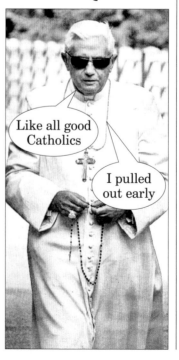

"We refuse to eat anything that's not locally grown"

"That's next-door's cat, isn't it?"

HUNTer

POPE QUITS!

Like all good Catholics

I pulled out early

POETRY CORNER

In Memoriam
Pope Benedict XVI

So. Farewell
Then,
Pope Benedict XVI.

You have decided
To take early
Retirement.

"In nomine Patris, et Filii, et Spiritus Sancti".
That was your catchphrase.

"Sieg Heil".
That was another
One from
An earlier time.

But we don't much
Mention that
Now.

E.J. Thribb (XVII½)

WE HAVE REASON TO BELIEVE THAT YOU HAVE BEEN RELABELLING HORSEMEAT, OLD MACDONALD

MOO MOO HERE

MOO MOO THERE

POLICE RAID

ROBERT THOMPSON

Greek tragedy rocks nation

BY E.U. RIPIDES

THE entire nation has been transfixed for weeks by the unfolding drama of the once powerful political leader Jashuhne and his vengeful spurned wife Medea-friendly.

The fall from grace of Jashuhne has been one of the most chilling political morality stories of our time.

Until only last year, Jashuhne dominated the national stage, after a dazzling career which had brought him both power and immense wealth.

His meteoric success was attributed by many of those who knew him to his glamorous Greek wife Medea-friendly, who made it possible for Jashuhne to amass a vast pile of gold by fleecing everybody he came across.

However, in a reckless moment of what Aristotle has described as "Huhnbris", Jashuhne fell madly in love with a young androgyne, half-woman, half-man, for whom he abandoned the marital home.

This drove his rejected wife into a paroxysm of fury and she summoned the dreaded harpies of the press to exact her revenge.

Ten years earlier, she revealed exclusively to the chief harpie of the Sunday Timons of Athens, her husband had been caught by the city's watchmen driving his chariot at 12 stades per hour in a 10sph zone on the main Argos to Athens chariotway.

Terrified that this would disqualify him from becoming Deputy Leader of the Argonauts, Jashuhne prevailed on his unhappy wife to pretend that she had been holding the reins of the chariot that night, when in fact she had been addressing a very important dinner of the Argos Women's Economic Forum on "Should we bring back the drachma?".

This revelation proved to be Jashuhne's downfall, or what Aristotle has called his "Libdemesis".

After only a year wondering what to do with the feuding couple, the city elders finally plucked up courage to put them on trial for the heinous crime that had now at last come to light.

Before the jury could place their pebbles in the urn, Jashuhne announced to the astonished people that he was entirely guilty and was prepared to resign from any further role in his country's state affairs, so long as he was let off.

At this point, to spite her husband, Medea produced her two children, who told the court that their father was an "f***** liar"and that they never wanted to see him again and that he would soon be consigned to spend an eternal life sentence in Hades.

On other pages

King Oedipus – "I could kill my father too" **3**
Clytemnestra – my love cheat hubby Agamemnon is even worse than Jashuhne **94**

The Eye's Controversial New Columnist

The columnist who refuses to take nappy-changing lying down

This week I am very angry about these so-called moaning moaners complaining about the proposed new high-speed rail link. Take my father, for example. He seemed to think that jumping up and down and screaming and waving his arms was enough to prevent the construction of my "Thomas the Tank Engine" railways network, which was specifically designed to solve the long-standing problem of transporting plastic chickens and cows from the bathroom, across the hall, through my bedroom and under the sofa. He seemed to think that, just because he had got a signal box imbedded in his foot, that this was grounds for abandoning the project altogether and *(cont. p. 94)*

school girl error,

THE EYE'S MOST READ STORIES

NHS issues strict new guidelines

The NHS says new guidelines issued to all nurses in the wake of the damning Mid Staffs report will make it clear they are only allowed to kill patients if they're really annoying.

"Just being old, a bit smelly and going on about the war all the time will no longer be a valid reason to kill a patient," said a senior NHS manager.

"Nurses will have to show that the patient is seriously getting on their tits big time before they'll be allowed to ice them.

"We will now be emphasising that every patient, no matter how annoying, deserves to be treated with dignity and respect, as they're being pulled across the ward by their hair and slowly starved to death."

HEALTH BOSS DEFENDS RECORD

The NHS isn't so bad – I've survived

NHS Direct

The gag reflex

What is the gag reflex?
It is the urge to gag anyone who might say something nasty about us.

How does it work?
It acts as a defence mechanism against any threat to the health of the organism (in this case, the NHS). The immediate reaction is to gag repeatedly until there is no further risk of damage and total immunity has been ensured.

Can it be overcome?
We'd prefer it if it wasn't, actually.

Are you sure?
I'd keep quiet if I was you or you'll be hearing from our lawyers.

Lookalikes

Twins   **Twins**

Sir,
Kray Twins/Cameron and Osborne...
JOHN JONES,
Via email.

Vicky Pryce   **Ed Byrne**

Sir,
I spotted this miscreant brumming around yesterday, yammering into his latest Carphone Warehouse purchase. Here's hoping the courts work efficiently and he receives the penalty endorsements he is due.
JOSH WHELAN,
Via email.

Pope   **Lagerfeld**

Sir,
Are they getting a new creative director at Chanel? I think we should be told.
G. GORDON-HALL,
Via email.

Simpson   **Farage**

Sir,
Every time I watch an episode of the Simpsons I feel I'm watching a UKIP party political broadcast; is it just the visual similarity or can there be something comical about Homer Simpson that I may have missed?
TIM MARTIN,
Via email.

Rennard   **Hill**

Sir,
I wonder if any of your readers have noticed the remarkable similarity between Benny Hill, who chased young women around so amusingly, and Lord Rennard, the Liberal Democrat peer? I wonder if, by any chance, they are related?
ENA B. WARNER-PUGH,
Via email.

Depardieu   **Neil**

Sir,
Perhaps you would like to place this recent picture of Andrew Neil beside one of Gérard Depardieu, the well-known journalist, in your pages?
HECTOR MARSHALL,
Via email.

Heavenly   **Heavenly**

Sir,
Has anyone noticed the resemblance of the young Archbishop of Canterbury, Justin Welby, whilst at Eton (as seen in the press recently), and the equally young Harry Styles of the popular singing group One Direction? Are they by any chance related?
Yours,
CARDINAL ENA B. NEWMAN,
Via email.

Jones   **Rubbisher**

Sir,
Inspired by your article on "Rubbisher of the Grauniad", I have found a lookalike at the Joanna.
ROGER ROBINSON-BROWN,
Via email.

Kate   **Evil Queen**

Sir,
Unable to sleep with this uncanny likeness(!!) thought you'd enjoy it... if we don't all end up in the Tower!!
SUZI HANNEY,
Via email.

Sir Edmund Hillary   **Rob Brydon**

Sir,
The resemblance is uncanny.
PAUL WAUDBY,
Via email.

Anne Atkins   **Ludwig van Beethoven**

Sir,
Are they by any chance related?
DAVID BECK,
Via email.

Picasso   **Cook**

Sir,
With the cricket season already upon us, I am surprised to find that the England captain (Alastair Cook) is easel-y (geddit?) confused with a young Pablo Picasso.
BRIAN POOLE,
Singapore.

Hilary Mantel   **Thomas Cromwell**

Sir,
You know what they say about dogs and their owners looking alike?
Don't you think that Hilary Mantel resembles very much her big love, Thomas Cromwell?

Regards,
CHERRI GILHAM,
Via email.

Hairy cornflake   **Hairy werewolf**

Sir,
Has anyone checked the dates of his Top of the Pops appearances to see if they coincide with a full moon?

JOHN MACGREGOR,
Via email.

Australian creature   **Blobfish**

Sir,
What do you make of these? One is an image of a bald miserable-looking Australian creature, and the other is a Blobfish (Psychrolutes marcidus).

MARK ELLIOTT,
Via email.

Dara   **Buzz**

Sir,
Have any of your readers noticed the remarkable similarity between the stand-up comedian Dara O'Briain and the Space Ranger hero of the Toy Story movies, Buzz Lightyear?

EVE WEST,
Sheffield.

John Bishop   **Barry Gibb**

Sir,
Can you explain how Barry Gibb morphed into John Bishop?

KATE JONES,
West Wickham.

Clinton   **Foot**

Sir,
Just wondered if anyone else spotted Hillary Clinton giving evidence yesterday to some committee or other over a bombing in Tripoli... She's turning into Michael Foot!

PHILIP DAVIES,
Via email.

Cherie   **Federico**

Sir,
Cherie Blair and Federico da Montefeltro, Duke of Urbino. One a Catholic humanist whose concern for the people promoted their loyalty and respect, the other, the wife of Tony Blair. Could they possibly be related?

RICHARD HAFFENDEN,
Address unknown.

Rory McIlroy   **Caravaggio's Boy**

Sir,
Amazing resemblance between this golfer and Caravaggio's "Boy Bitten By A Scorpion" in the National Gallery.

Regards,
DAVID SPOMMERLAD,
Brill, Bucks.

Cameron   **Berlusconi**

Sir,
Related?
ROGER SHORT,
Via email.

Earl Wonga   **John Humphrys**

Sir,
I knew that Nicholas Parsons had sold his soul to Wonga for the voiceovers on their Ads on TV, but did not realise that Earl is in fact John Humphrys! However, Earl... er sorry, John does brush up well when he needs to receive an award, don't you think? Keep up the good work.

Best Regards,
MICHAEL SKINLEY,
Via email.

Christine   **Quentin**

Sir,
I could not help noticing the similarity between the late Quentin Crisp, the Naked Civil Servant, and Christine Lagarde, the Managing Director of the International Monetary Fund. Both known experts on austerity, could they possibly be related?

CAROLINE DAVIS,
Via email.

Johnson   **Roman God**

Sir,
The recent discovery of a Roman God in County Durham bears a startling resemblance to Boris Johnson.

SIMON GREEN,
Via email.

DAILY EXPRESS

54% OF LONDON FOXES 'COME FROM BULGARIA'

A SHOCK new report commissioned by the Daily Express has found that OVER HALF the foxes living illegally in the capital are from Bulgaria *(cont. p. 94)*

How to spot a Bulgarian fox in London

They are:
- scruffy and unkempt
- often seen rummaging through bins
- fairly hopeless at speaking English when challenged

EXCLUSIVE TO ALL TORY PAPERS

THOSE VITAL QUESTIONS NICK CLEGG MUST ANSWER NOW OR RESIGN

1 When did he know about the specific allegations against Lord Rennard?

2 Why didn't he act quickly to investigate the women's allegations?

3 When did he know that Lord Rennard was fat?

4 Why does he deny that Lord Rennard is an anagram of Savile Loving Pervert?

5 When did he hear about people asking him when he knew what he'd heard he'd known?

6 When did he first hear our earlier question about Lord Rennard being a fatty?

7 Where was he when Kennedy was assassinated?

8 Which Shakespeare play ends with Alcibiades reading the title character's epitaph and promising to bring peace to that character's home city?

9 The Lost Stradivarius and The Nebuly Coat are two of John Meade Falkner's three published novels. Which work, published in 1898, is the third?

10 Why hasn't Clegg resigned despite failing to answer specific and detailed questions put to him by us in the hope that he would lose the by-election and *(That's enough, Ed.)*

"ARE YOU FROM ATOS?"

THE AAA RATING
An Apology

IN RECENT weeks, in common with all other newspapers, we may have given the impression that nothing was more important to the international standing and financial reputation of the United Kingdom than the fact that it has continued to receive a AAA rating from prestigious authorities such as Moody's. We may further have given readers to believe that the entire future of the UK economy depended on Britain continuing to enjoy this supreme mark of financial reliability, particularly at a time when many other countries, such as the USA and France, were being humiliatingly stripped of their AAA status and becoming economic pariahs shunned and distrusted by the world markets.

We now realise, in the light of Britain's financial standing having been demoted by Moody's to its AA1 status, that these attempts to "rate" complex economies according to the mercurial whims of a few overpaid employees of such self-important and vastly over-rated bodies as Moody's are wholly meaningless and should be brushed aside with all the contempt they deserve.

We would further like to make it clear that we are now delighted that the UK has once again been accorded its rightful place in the world alongside such vibrant and dynamic economies as those of the US, France, Italy, Spain, Greece and Zimbabwe. *(Is this right? Ed.)*

 Dave Snooty AND HIS NEW PALS

GEORGE HAS MESSED UP HIS SUMS AGAIN! HE'S HAVING A THRASHING FROM MR MOODY!

IS THAT GOOD OR BAD?

THWACK!

MATHS REPORT 0/10

YAA1ROOOO!!!

GEORGE DOESN'T KNOW HIS AAAS FROM HIS ELBOW!

THUD!

NO, YOU'VE GOT TO GIVE OSBO SOME CREDIT...

'COS NOBODY ELSE WILL, EH, READERS?!? HAAA HAAA HAAA!

SO WHY DON'T YOU GIVE OSBO THE BOOT EH, DAVE???

BECAUSE THEN **I'D** BE THE MOST USELESS MEMBER OF THE GANG!!!

HOOR - A A 1!!!

GLENDA SLAGG

She's 100% cow!!! (Geddit?!)

■ JEREMY IRONS – Ok, so he likes a bit of slap and tickle with the young babes on the film set!?! So what??? What red-blooded gal wouldn't want to have TV's Pope Borgia a-fumblin' and a-fondlin' her dainty derrière!!! It's just a bit of harmless fun, all you prudes out there, and that's the bottom line!!!?

■ JEREMY IRONS – Urgggghh!!! You're a disgrace, grandad, as you go a-gropin' and a-grabbin' at any glamorous gal within arm's reach??!? Lock up your daughters everyone, because TV's Pervy Pope has a hands-on approach to film-making??!? Harmless fun??? As excuses go, Mr Jerry-attrick (geddit??!), that's Rock Bottom (geddit???!)

■ HATS (and trousers) off to Hugh Grant!!!? The floppy-haired film star has had another little 'un!!! All together now... Ahhhh!??! And what's the dotin' dad gonna call his beautiful bouncing boy??!? Not Rupert – that's for sure?!? How about Lord Leveson Grant??!? That's gotta kinda ring to it – and not the phone you can hack into?!?! (Geddit???!)

■ HUGH GRANT – What a disgrace!!!? The floppy-haired philanderer has fathered yet another sprog with his so-called "fleeting fancy", Ms Chop Suey (Check, subs)!?! No wonder we're all hacked off with Hugh, an irresponsible, one-man population explosion!! Love Actually??!? I don't think so!!?! More like "Luvvies Actually"!??! Or should it be "No Weddings and Another Christening"??!? Talk about an upper-class Twitter!!!?

PS. Please don't report me to Lord Leveson, Hughie, I'm a big fan really!!?!??

■ MARY BEARD – Don'tchaluv-her??!? She's the oldie pin-up of the year, the classical cutie that's got Britain's Latin lovers all weak at the knees (and I don't mean their arthritis!!!). She's the pouting prof with the luscious locks in fifty shades of grey!!? Geddit???! Her tales of her raunchy past are the best kind of ancient history lesson!!?? What a classic act??!?

■ MARY BEARD – Aren'tchasick-ofher?? Oldie pin-up?! Oldie "shut up" more like!!? Put a sock in it, Granny – we don't want to hear about your ancient history and your classical conquests back in BC years??!! Go back to your ivory tower, Beardie, and lock yourself in??!? Geddit!!?? PS. Please don't get me arrested for trolling, Prof, just making the fair point that you are a bit ubiquitous at the moment. No offence!!?!

■ Had an audience with Queen Helen Mirren yet??! Me neither zzzzzzz.

■ HERE THEY ARE – Glenda's Mad March Hairies?!?!

● Ben Affleck!?!! You're the bearded Bafta winner who directed Argo!?! Come and have Argo at Glenda if you think you're up to it??!? Geddit???!

● George Clooney!?!! You're the bearded Bafta winner who produced Argo!!?? Come and have Argo at Glenda if you think *(You've done this. Ed.)*

● The other bearded bloke who won the Bafta!?!! Crazy beard, crazy guy!?!!

Byeee!!

Those ten tell-tale questions the Vicky Pryce jury asked the judge

1. Your Honour, we've heard a lot during this case about "the Lib Dems". Who or what are they?

2. Some of us were reminded of the plot of a recent Midsomer Murders. Are we allowed to base our verdict on that?

3. Is it a reasonable inference to decide that Miss Pryce must be innocent because her husband's new girlfriend looks like Wendolene out of Wallace and Gromit?

4. Does a majority verdict mean that most of us have to agree one way or another and how many is a majority out of twelve? Is it all twelve?

5. What is "marital coalition"? This one's got us really stumped!

6. If we can't make up our minds on a verdict, will we go to jail for contempt of court, as it says on Wikipedia?

7. One of us was talking in the pub the other night to a guy who said he'd once fitted a new kitchen for the Huhnes and his opinion was that she was really nice and that it would be really unfair to send her to jail. Are we allowed to rely on this as evidence?

8. If Mr Huhne is sentenced to time in prison, can he force his wife to serve the sentence for him?

9. Could you tell us, Your Honour, whether you think Mrs Huhne is guilty or not? This would really help us to make up our minds and then we can all go home.

10. Why doesn't the picture in the paper look anything like us?

Hands off our journalists, officer.

No – literally. Could you please not arrest me? I've got a leader column to write about how shameful it is that News International journalists are being picked on by the Police in a series of punitive raids, stage-managed by the Police to counteract the bad publicity they got over Plebgate and Hillsborough. Ouch! Sorry officer, I didn't mean to bring that up again, but you are being a bit heavy-handed. I don't remember discussing this over lunch. How about this brown envelope of cash? No? We're not doing that anymore? And of course – you never did.

THE SUN SAYS
No please, not the Taser. Aaaaaaargh!

CARDINAL IN SEX SHOCK

Let us prey

OF COURSE PATRICK, YOU DON'T ACTUALLY HAVE TO BANISH THE SNAKES! MOVING THEM FROM PARISH TO PARISH SHOULD SUFFICE

A great and respected institution... tarnished by evidence of sex abuse and cover-up... But enough of the BBC – we turn now to the Catholic Church...

Oscars Frocks Shocks!

IT'S OSCAR TIME AGAIN... and our rancid fashion editor **LIZ BONES** applauds the appropriately attired and snubs the sartorially second-rate!

Adele's dress is **Bond** to set hearts racing! **Spy** reckon she has a licence to thrill in this sexy black number! If she wants to **Roger Moore**, she's certainly going to get her wish! They'll be **Q**-ing round the block!

Oh-oh-dear! **Blow(feld)** me down and get a **Sky-fall** of this monstrosity! *(This is nonsense. Ed.)* Next time, spend a bit of **Moneypennies** on a designer who can do a proper **Odd-Job**!

Spy wonder what made Jessica put this on? *(You've done this one. Ed.)* **Water torture** to see her in this horrible frock! **Terror** I'll slap her **rist** if she wears it again! *(What? Ed.)*

Jessica is looking a real blonde **bombshell**!! All in **al**, this is my **Qaeda** dress! I give this **Nine** out of **Eleven**! This gown will **ensure gents** flock to her side (insurgents, geddit?)! *(You're mad. Ed.)*

Halle-o fellahs! What a **Berry** nice dress this is! I'm sure a lot of her **x-men** wish they weren't tonight! She's **Bond** to be in for a **monster ball**, and that dress will live to **dye another day**. *(This isn't Halle Berry, you silly cow. Ed.)*

The **first** thing this **lady** should have done is not wear this dress! Those earrings with that frock? Talk about a **state of the union**! I'm gonna **Barack** her until she sees **cents**! *(Drones have been despatched. Ed.)*

DIARY

MY FAVOURITE BOWIE

ALAN TITCHMARSH: Whether you enjoyed *Ziggy Stardust* more than *Scary Monsters* is really a matter for you, but whichever you plump for, I sincerely trust you found something to enjoy in both, because there's certainly plenty to celebrate. David Bowie is a lovely chap who's provided us with bags of memorable music, and given us all a great deal of pleasure as well as some great lyrics to keep us guessing! In my view, he's well up there with some of the true legends of popular music, such as Cliff Richard, The Swingle Singers and the evergreen Chris de Burgh. I hear that his new album has got a bit of everything, and many things in between (!), so plump up the cushions, get the kettle on, pin back the old lug-holes and... enjoy!

PROFESSOR RICHARD DAWKINS: In this day and age, it's hard to believe anyone would be so woefully ignorant of the universe as to believe there's a starman waiting in the sky, and, furthermore, that he told us not to blow it because he knows it's all worthwhile. It's quite simply preposterous.

PAUL MORLEY: It's albeit impossible to characterise, transcribe or otherwise personifiy the zeitgeist-breaking role that *Jean Genie* occupies, plays or otherwise engages in with the post-modern zeitgeist that is Britain now but ultimately it's a tremendously complex expression of the zeitgeist and not only *of* the zeitgeist but *for* the zeitgeist because in an extraordinary sort of way and to an unprecedented extent in the history of modern music, the remaining elements begin to have a life of their own and continue the lonely search for new ideas about form and formation, decay and growth, mystery and consciousness as single-mindedly as Stockhausen, all of which makes ultimately it very relevant to the zeitgeist of today.

THE RT HON NICK CLEGG: Let's move away from the whole thing of saying this Bowie song is better than that Bowie song. That's the old way, and – you know what? – it has never worked. No: together, we must sit down and work out a new way to tackle this whole question. I believe passionately that this is a goal we should all work towards, and that's why it's high on my agenda. I hope that answers your question. If it doesn't, I can only say one thing. I am well and truly sorry.

JULIAN FELLOWES: In truth, *Lady Grinning Soul* should be more properly addressed as The Dowager Countess of Grinning Soul, as she is the wife of the late Earl of Grinning Soul, and consequently the mother of the present Earl, who, incidentally, proved a rich source of inspiration when I was creating the immortal role of the scheming Jemima, Duchess of Weston-Super-Mare in Downton last season. I was, to my great delight, placed next to The Dowager Countess of Grinning Soul at a rather jolly luncheon with local aristocracy the other day – we keep it firmly under wraps, but my wife is fearfully grand! – and I may say she informed me, in no uncertain terms, that Mr Bowie is *persona non grata* in their household, oh, very much so, as one should never sing in public about "the fullness of her breast" when everyone knows the correct word to use is *embonpoint*.

As told to CRAIG BROWN

HEIR OF SORROWS
A Short Story Special

by Dame Sylvie Krin, author of *Duchess of Hearts* & *You're Never Too Old*

IN LAST WEEK'S HEIR OF SORROWS: Charles was listening to the radio in the bath and mistakenly got the impression that his mother was going to abdicate when, in fact, it was Queen Beatrix of the Netherlands. Severe disappointment ensued. Now read on...

"AND how is our bath, sire?" The silky tones of Sir Alan Fitztightly soothed Charles' agitated frame of mind.

"It really is... appealing," Charles replied, luxuriating in the Duchy Original Wattle 'n' Daub Organic Bath Balm.

"Would sire care for the radio?"

Did Charles detect a hint of amusement in Sir Alan's voice? A wry reference to the unfortunate events of his previous bath?

"Yes, I would, actually." Charles refused to be cowed by the eminent Rouge Dragon Pursuivant in his buckskin breeches.

"And make sure it stays on Radio 4 this time – none of that ghastly Radio 3 World Music thingie... I mean, that really is..."

"Appalling, sire?"

Sir Alan turned on the brand new Trevor Bailey wind-up radio, a safe replacement for the digital Andrew Roberts model which had previously dropped into the bath and unceremoniously exploded.

"Let's turn you on, Your Maj, shall we... as Backstairs Billy used to say in the old days of your dear, departed Nan."

"Yes, thank you, Sir Alan. That will be all." Charles dismissed the smirking Keeper of the Royal Loofah and lay back to listen to the mellow tones of continuity announcer Theo Walcott.

"And now, more on the story of the leader of the church who has suddenly resigned to make way for a younger man."

Charles leapt excitedly out of the bath, the shampoo suds streaming from his head like a crown of *(cont. p. 94)*

A very human tragedy

by Our Prisons Correspondent
Phil Bucket

Well-wishers took to the airwaves to commiserate with prominent Lib Dem MP Nick Clegg, who was sentenced to two more years as leader of the Liberal Democrats yesterday.

"He was a real high-flyer," said one family friend, "and his political career is now in ruins just because of one stupid little mistake, standing for leadership of the Liberal Democrats."

Chris Huhne said, "I don't want to dwell on what is a very personal tragedy for him and his family. Just think, but for a quirk of fate, it could be me as leader of the Liberal Democrats and him enjoying the limelight as a respected jailbird.

"I think it's best that Nick spends the next couple of years out of the public eye in an attempt to make people forget that he is leader of the Liberal Democrats."

HUHNE/PRYCE JAILED
Those two terms in full

Harpie

Bastard

GLENDA SLAGG

She's the gal who is really ****ed off! Geddit??!!

■ BOO HOO Huhne!?!! Spare a tear for poor old Vicky Pryce wearing a suit with arrows on it as she sits in Cell Block H sewing mailbags. And for why!? Just because she took her revenge on two-timing love rat hubby Chris!! What red-blooded gal *wouldn't* have dished the dirt on the loudmouth LibDem lothario??!! Eight months!?! She should have been given a medal or made a Dame for services to the sisterhood!!?!

■ BOO HOO Huhne!?! This gal ain't wasting any tears on vengeful Vicky the harridan from hell as she sits in her cushy country house en-suite prison a-trimmin' and a-strimmin' the roses in the garden!?! What type of cold-blooded harpy plots to ruin the father of her kiddies and bring shame on the whole family!?!! No wonder charismatic Chris dumped her for cutie Carina!?! Eight months?!? She should have been given the death penalty!?? (No offence, Vicky, are we still on for that girls' trip to Greece to write your memoirs – all on exes, promise?!!!)

■ ERIC Joyce – OK, so he likes a drop and then enjoys a fight afterwards!?!! Who doesn't!? Lighten up, Mr Prudish Pressman

– we need an MP who adds a bit of colour to drab, dull old Westminster??!! He's the people's Joyce (geddit!?!) and we would rather he was in the bars than behind them!!?! (Geddit!?!)

■ ERIC Joyce – what a disgrace!?!! He's the fighting Falkirk MP who can't hold his drink or keep his temper!?!! If you can't have a debate without resorting to fisticuffs, then you're better off behind bars than in them!!?! (Geddit!?!)

■ **HERE THEY ARE – Glenda's Leveson Loverboys?!?!**

● **Hugh Grant!?!!** Mmm!!?! He's striking a blow-job for press freedom !?! (Geddit!!?!)

● **Professor Brian Cathcart!?!!** He's Hugh's friend, the dandruffed don, stoopid!?! Come and gag this gal anytime!!?!

● **Evan Harris!?!!** He's the other one who hangs around with Hacked-Off Hugh and the Pouting Prof!! I'll sleep with Evan you!?!!

● **Lord Leveson!?!!** Crazy name, very sensible recommendations (in part), your Lordship.

Byeee!!

"Hi – I'm de-cluttering"

DEIRDRE SPART (Leading Feminist and Author of Seminal New Work *Lean Left*)

Once again, we have been forced to witness the sexist humiliation of a totally innocent woman by the forces of the patriarchial judicio-genderist establishment, ie the jailing of Vicky Pryce who, as an independent career woman in her own right, had no option but to submit to the orders of her fascist Lib Dem husband, viz she was maritally coerced by the totally unreconstructed male chauvinist pig Huhne... er... and furthermore she was sickeningly discriminated against when a male judge sentenced her to the same punishment as Huhne who, as a male, should have been given a much harsher penalty, ie castration, due to his running off with that awful woman who is not a patch on my old friend Vicky and it's all jolly unfair, er...

"What can we do for you today, sir?"

THIS WEEK

LORD AHMED

Do spoons play an important part in your life?

They do. I am very lucky to have a lot of spoons, which thankfully senior Jewish figures have not yet been able to confiscate from me.

Why do you like spoons so much?

My Jewish friends in the establishment will assert that it's because I am using them for my own dark practices. In fact, I simply like a good spoon.

Do you have a favourite spoon?

My favourite spoons are all kept under lock and key in case senior British judges, who also happen to be Jews, should have me arrested on trumped-up charges and confiscate them.

Did you miss your spoons when you were in prison for dangerous driving?

This is exactly the sort of foolish comment that marks you out as a friend of the global Jewish plan to dominate the media, the judiciary, and the World Spoon Federation.

Has anything amusing ever happened to you in connection with a spoon?

No.

(Translated for Private Eye from the original Urdu)

NEXT WEEK: *Britney Spears: Me and My Spears.*

Lord Luvvieson's Report
HISTORIC FUDGE AGREED

It's an end to press harassment!

Now will you leave us alone?

'Victims must decide the law' says Miliband

by Our Political Staff
Sharia Law

THE Labour leader, Mr Ed Milibandwagon, today announced a historic new departure for the British legal system.

Following on from his meeting with Hugh Grant, of the pressure group Hackety-hack-hack-hacked-off, which represents victims of the press, Mr Milibandwagon said, "It is up to the victims of crime to decide on the penalties for the perpetrators and on the exact details of the framework for regulation. Unless of course the victims are victims of the NHS, the banking system, or the political process... when they should have nothing to do with it, obviously... not to mention the victims of paedophiles and murderers who probably want the guilty to be strung up, as it's the only language they understand, and we can't have that."

Mr Milibandwagon then said, "There is a clear lesson to be learned here. Don't allow me to open my mouth in public."

Mr Milibandwagon is 27.

DAVE SPART (Co-Chair of the Tufnell Park Pro-Tidal-Windfarm Anti-Fracking Save-The-Badger-Not-The-Bankers Socialist Alliance)

It is sickeningly predictable that the British government have yet again imposed their will on the defenceless Malvinas islands by the nauseating premise of holding a sham "election" when there were no votes for those proud Argentinians who would have been living on the islands if they had only been allowed to by the fascist junta run by Mrs Thatcher and her lickspittle running dogs who, er, and also totally predictably there were no votes given to the millions of noble Malvinas penguins, so resentful of their hated British overlords yet so cruelly disenfranchised by simple discrimination on grounds of species and height... Er... The fact that the overwhelming majority of people voted for the islands to remain a British protectorate is just further proof – as if it were needed – that the election was rigged – rigged like the British warships which barbarously evicted the proud Argentinians in 1833, despite the fact that Argentina didn't exist at the time... er...

DR WHO PERVY '80s PRODUCER

He asked me to go upstairs

BRITISH PRESS AWARDS HIGHLIGHTS

The Oscars of British journalism are presented in front of an audience comprising the cream of Fleet Street

Presenter: And sadly the winner of "Reporter of the Year" can't be here tonight because he's in jail. And so is the runner-up. But highly-commended is... No – apparently she's been arrested as well. But here to collect the award on her behalf is Detective Inspector Dawn Raid of Operation Jailhack.

Detective Inspector *(in tears)*: I'd like to thank all my colleagues. It's not just me. It's the whole force...

Presenter: I'm sorry, I'll have to cut you off there, Dawn, because one of your colleagues, Detective Inspector Nick Copper of Operation Freelunch, is waiting in the wings to arrest you for selling your story about accepting an award to a tabloid paper.

Detective Inspector: It's a fair cop.

Presenter: Moving on, we now come to "Newspaper of the Year". And the newspaper of the year is... No longer operating because it's been closed down. So on to "Scoop of the Year". This was a sensational story, covered by all the newspapers every week. And it was... "Journalists Arrested". So please could you all put your hands together...

Audience: We already have – they're in handcuffs.

WE'LL HAVE NO TROUBLE HERE, THEIR BORDER AGENCY'S NOT FIT FOR PURPOSE

Cluff

Mrs May Abolishes UK Borders

by Our Political Staff
Peter Oborder

In a spectacular bid for the Tory leadership, Theresa May, the Home Secretary, last night moved to solve the immigration crisis at a stroke.

"The UK Border Agency was clearly failing," she said, "so what I had to do was simply abolish the UK Borders. Now there is no longer any need to keep a record of who's coming into the country.

"This way, there is no backlog of illegal immigrants, we will no longer see those embarrassing figures telling us that another million people, equivalent to the size of the population of Birmingham, have arrived on a lorry – and we no longer need to worry about all those 29 million Bulgarians and Romanians who can now come over whenever they like."

A meeting of Tory back-benchers expressed a warm welcome for Mrs May's imagination and tough near-solution to the "migrant problem", but said that they would be voting for Boris as leader anyway.

Nursery Times

Friday, Once-upon-a-time

'I'M OFF' SAYS DISAPPOINTED DEE, AS HE DESERTS DUM

By Our Political Staff **Michael White Rabbit**

THE MOST famous double-act in Nurseryland fell dramatically apart last night when Tweedledee threw his toys out of the pram and headed off for foreign climes.

"I don't want to be a distraction, particularly if my little brother becomes Chief Rattle Holder after the next election and everyone keeps saying how much better a job holding the rattle I would do."

Tweedledee is leaving the Mad Hattersley Tea Party. He said, "The whole thing's become like a pantomime, with the audience shouting to my brother 'He's behind you' every time I appear, when quite obviously I'm not behind him."

Career Behind You

Tweedledum paid handsome tribute to his brother, saying, "It's a very great loss to Nurseryland and I shall miss the sound of his rattle hitting me over the head, while he shouts 'Contrariwise' every time I come up with a new policy."

Tweedledee is reported to be leaving Nurseryland to take up a lucrative new post helping poor refugees like the Three Little Pigs, who were forced to flee their homes after they were blown down in a series of wolf-related disasters.

Mr Plod Announces More Celebrity Arrests

By **Eve Ningall**

IN AN expansion of Operation YewToo, Mr Plod today swooped on the home of Seventies TV favourite Mr Tickle. Mr Tickle instantly rejected the charges, saying, "Things were very different then. It was entirely innocent, and I meant no harm – it's just what I do."

It is now thought that Mr Tickle was one of a group of men known as the "Mr Men". A delighted Mr Plod said, "We are casting the net even wider now, in the hope of destroying all the happy memories of childhood that we can."

Mr Happy was said to be very upset.

Scan reveals clot behind Hillary Clinton's right ear

haven't you finished Kindle yet?
You've been reading it for months

BORIS FOUND DEAD
Was he murdered or was it suicide?

by Our Crime Staff **Hugh Dunnit**

An ever-growing air of mystery surrounds the bizarre death of the colourful, controversial figure of Boris Trousersofsky, who met his end in "unexplained circumstances" in a BBC studio last Sunday morning.

When Boris was first discovered slumped in a crumpled heap on the set of the Sunday morning show "Nobody's Watching", it was assumed that he was the victim of an assassin.

Eddie Mair of London

The word quickly went round that Boris had been targeted by a professional hit man, Eddie Mairderer, who used deadly weapons such as old accusations of lying and infidelity and who had been put up to the crime by shadowy figures surrounding Britain's ruthless dictator David "Vlad" Camerof.

"Dave's fingerprints were all over this," said one highly-placed security source. "He's always hated Boris for being more popular than him and has increasingly seen him as a threat."

But the more that comes to light about the peculiar circumstances of Boris's dramatic end, the more likely it seems that his death was in fact suicide.

Said one forensic expert, "The supposed assassin just gave Boris the rope, and then he hanged himself."

Meanwhile, tributes to the deceased are still pouring in from every part of the political spectrum.

One venerable figure who was associated with Boris for many years, "Red Ken" Leninspart, said, his eyes glistening with tears of joy, "This is truly a tragic end to a golden career. Now can I be Mayor again, please?"

EXCLUSIVE TO ALL NEWSPAPERS

BEREZOVSKY – WAS HIS DEATH DUE TO A KREMLIN MURDER PLOT?

We don't know.

THE JOHNSONS

"Oh no – it's that comedy family who are on all the time!"

Why Europe is once again on the brink of war (and why this could cause a collapse in house prices)

by Top Mail Historian
Phil Spacebrook

MAKE no mistake. The parallels between what is happening in Europe today and what was happening exactly 100 years ago are both uncanny and chilling.

In 1913 no one realised that within twelve months the entire world would be engulfed by a conflagration such as had never been seen before in history.

Then, as now, an overmighty Germany was bestriding the continent like a colossus, dictating terms to its weaker neighbours such as Greece, Spain and Italy.

Then, as now, an upper-class British prime minister was dithering, helplessly, unable to act decisively in face of all the crises clustering around his government.

Then, as now, the British people continued to take refuge from reality in an endless round of glittering society balls and celebrity TV reality shows.

Then, as now, our country was quite literally dancing on the edge of the precipice of a mighty

abyss, blissfully oblivious to the catastrophe that was bearing down on them with the speed of the iceberg that had destroyed the supposedly unsinkable Titanic only a year before. *(Keep this going. This is just what I wanted. P.D.)*

Perhaps the most startling parallel of all is the extraordinary physical similarity between Germany's present "Iron Chancellor" Frau Angela Merkel and that country's then ruler, Kaiser Wilhelm II.

Not only were their imperialistic ambitions disturbingly similar, but, as our pictures show, the current author of Europe's economic woes is the living twin of the man who launched the world into a conflict

that was to leave 30 million people dead.

And what was even worse than the loss of life, as a whole generation was wiped out almost overnight, was the Europe-wide collapse in EU house prices (particularly on the Franco-Belgian border), which was to plunge the continent into a state of economic meltdown that would lead inexorably to the rise of Hitler and the horrors of World War Two.

And it is about to happen again.

People will say, "This is a bit far-fetched. Surely things aren't quite as bad as that?"

Well, all I can say, as a respected Daily Mail historian, is "Yes, I'm afraid the picture is even worse than the one I have painted. If history can tell us one thing it is that this sort of piece is worth a couple of thousand quid from the Daily Mail." *(Great stuff, Phil. Same again tomorrow. P.D.)*

Murder retrial demanded

by Our News Correspondent,
Jim 'Foxy' Naughtie

A RETRIAL of the notorious 2007 murder case in Perugia has been demanded. Particularly by the press, who want the chance to reprint all the salacious details again and fill their papers with large photos of Foxy Knoxy, but not any photos of the bloke with specs, because we don't care whether he's innocent or not, because, let's face it, he's not very foxy, is he?

"I give up"

Mail Online

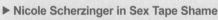

Pope Frock Shock!

Our Fashion Editor, Liz Bones, takes on the papal briefs and gives us the winners and losers on the Vatican catwalk...

Talk about **mass** appeal, this stunning white number is a winner! Papal bully for you, Francis. If you're aiming to be top of the Popes **rite** now, your chances are looking **rosary**.

What a **cardinal** error. I don't want to **pontificate**, but this boring white number won't win any **converts**. It's all so old hat and I don't mean that thing on your head, Benedict! *(You're fired. Ed.)*

Notes&queries

The meeting of two popes

● The Reverend Hornbeam is quite wrong to suggest that the meeting of Francis I and Benedict XVI was the first meeting of two Popes in 600 years. Any reasonably informed Vaticanologist would know that Pope Innocent the Smoothie met Pope Idol (formerly Simon the Cowell) in 1578 at the so-called Conference of Rihanna, where Pope Idol stood down after losing an argument over which day of the week Good Friday should fall on, thus proving his fallibility and ensuring his replacement by Pope Innocent (formerly Cardinal Error).
Mrs Ludmilla Widdecombe of Strictly-cum-Dancing, Dorset.

● Mrs Widdecombe is both correct and incorrect – correct on the history, but incorrect on the theology. Surely all Popes meet their predecessors in heaven, one would imagine, on their first day of arrival? On this basis, the last time two Popes met was obviously in 2005 when Pope John Paul II met John Paul I. No doubt the recording angel has made a note of it...
That's enough – Ed.

Answers please:

Which direction does One Direction refer to?
What was Hugh Grant's profession before he entered politics?
What is the maximum number of dips in a recession?

"We believe that you may have been missold PPI and may be eligible for compensation..."

"He can watch pornography as long as I can censor it"

Daily Mail, Friday, March 22, 2013

PAEDO PIT TO CLOSE

by Our Broadcasting Staff
Claire Monger

THERE was widespread joy throughout Britain today as the BBC Paedo Pit in West London, also known as TV Centre, closed its doors for the last time.

Opened in 1960 as a special pervert drop-in centre where Jimmy Savile and thousands of other BBC paedos from around Britain would be able to come together to abuse children under the one roof, the Paedo Pit quickly gained a reputation with paedophiles worldwide as being the preeminent location for both live and recorded kiddy- fiddling in Britain.

Over the next 50 years of sickening non-stop abuse within its walls, the BBC Paedo Pit in West London came to be a symbol of everything that was truly wretched about everything everywhere.

TELLY TALK

BBC to celebrate historic closure

The BBC has announced a series of programmes to celebrate the closure of a filing cabinet in West London.

"To many people who don't work in television, this filing cabinet is just another piece of office furniture," said a misty-eyed BBC staffer,

"but the reality is that it's far more than that, this filing cabinet has been right at the heart of broadcasting for almost fifty years.

"The heritage of this cabinet runs right from classic shows such as "Only Fools and Horses", when David Jason may have once leant on the cabinet, right through to "The Office", as Ricky Gervais' hit show had lots of cabinets in it that looked a bit like this one, and "Miranda", as she's thought to have tripped and fallen over one.

A star-studded three-hour

"Goodbye to the Filing Cabinet Special" to be broadcast on BBC2 on April 19th will feature many of Britain's most loved and respected TV presenters, talking about how much they loved the filing cabinets and why it shouldn't be closely followed by a live concert in the park from Madness.

BBC to make TV programme for television

There was widespread astonishment in the broadcasting world today after the BBC confirmed plans to show the new Peter Kay sitcom on the television.

"Obviously, we'd prefer to BitTorrent the comedy directly onto Twitter via a PS3 link downloaded from the iPlayer streaming a podcast directly on the viewer's iPad," said the BBC's head of digital virtual integration and platform virtual content (£105,000 pa), Jeremy Googleglass.

"But, strangely, our market research tells us people would really just prefer to watch it on the telly."

DIARY

BRIAN SEWELL

Mao Tse Tung: that last name says it all. "Tung by name, Tung by nature" I noted, a mite waspishly, when, upon one day, I awoke to find that busy little mite of a Chairman, as he insisted so improbably upon being addressed, still clad in his neatly-pressed blue romper suit, gingerly nibbling upon my genitalia as one might on an under-dressed crab at a luncheon party thrown for the disgraced second cousin of a minor Marquess, just back from one of the less salubrious suburbs of Buenos Aires.

Where exactly into one another Tung and I had first bumped is not a question upon which I intend for too long to dwell. The memory is fraught for me with the disagreeable whiff of his boorish sanctimony and feeble attempts at "opinions". Though singularly brutish, foul and hideous to the point of venality, Beijing is a city, if it can be so described, blessed with all manner of nooks and crannilaculari, each one available for whistle-stop copulation, but none worthy of the effort of recollection. May it suffice to say that after the muted urgency of our first coupling, Tung insisted upon having me up against the Great Wall.

Alas and, as it were, alack, his banal Red Book was not the only thing about the Chairman I found to be Little. His little gargoyle was a byword in stubbiness, less monument than matchstick, and peculiarly ill-fitting: a piece of ill-luck that no amount of public posturing – oh, the infinite tedium of that dreary Long March! – could ever hope to disguise.

I told Tung, no spring chicken himself, "Towards the beginning of the Nineteen Seventies, I enjoyed, though the more apposite past participle would be 'underwent', a somewhat hurried liaison in the back of a singularly ramshackle vehicle with your portly chum, that silver-haired lickspittle Teddy Heath. He was, as I recall, Prime Minister at the time, though it was an office whose correct pronunciation he could, for all his futile ambition, never quite master"

Tung leaned close to my beautifully shampooed locks and spluttered damply into my ear – how repelled I still feel by the infernal drip-drip-drip of his spittle on my lobe! – that he had once fucked Giscard d'Estaing in the back of a horse-drawn carriage as it cruised, as one does, down the Avenue des Champs-Elysees.

I told him that I had undergone only the briefest of flings with Giscard, and had found him too bony. In terms both forthright and vehement, Tung disagreed: he clearly still bore a candle for him, and much else besides. To a man, the French have always enjoyed being taken from behind in public places by tubby Orientals of a domineering persuasion. De Gaulle was the same, I hear.

Barely halfway through November, and Christmas rears its sluttish little visage once more. I can think of only one Christmas I ever enjoyed, and that in the late 1950s, when, as an undistinguished Grandfather clock struck midnight with shrill insolence, I found myself being ignominiously but not unpleasurably gang-banged up the rear by three battalions of Horse Guards, an off-duty policeman, eleven pipers piping, ten lords-a-leaping, the Admissions committee of the Courtauld Institute, and the first, second, third, fourth and fifth men, and all in association with Messrs Knight, Frank and positively my least favourite, that ghastly lickspittle, Rutley.

Since then, the steadiness with which things have gone not uphill but down, is barely worth the breath necessary for enunciating a comment. Only last year, for example, I paid a visit to Santa's Grotto at a Department Store in Oxford Street. Upon easing myself onto the visibly yearning knees of the florid, ill-shaven Claus, I became steadily more aware of the pure bile of jealousy and hatred oozing from the pores of the children, asinine and presumptuous, who howled and wailed in a monstrous queue stretching back some several hundred yards.

It was upon asking Claus for a modest present of cash in hand – notes only – that he revealed himself as a vile, arrogant and ignorant old martinet with hands ready less to dip deep into his own pockets than into mine.

"Bah! Away with you, you foul, gushing taradiddle, you loathsome poltroon!" I said, perfectly reasonably. But these people have no manners, no manners at all. The worthless, puce-faced ogre accordingly summoned an obese security guard, and together they manhandled me out of their dreary little shop, while their underage hangers-on continued with their bawling and blubbering.

Whither the Christmases of years gone by, whither the largesse, the bonhomie, the festive cheer and merriment? Abandoned, methinks, to the shallow brouhaha of this unhappy age!

As told to CRAIG BROWN

Unworkable, Badly Thought Through Law to be Introduced to Halt Introduction of Unworkable, Badly Thought Through Laws

by Our Political Staff
Dominic Lawsoff

Following a rash of unworkable, badly thought through laws regarding immigrants, the press, the health service, schools, tax, VAT, media ownership, and disability welfare, the Prime Minister has announced the introduction of an unworkable, badly thought through law to ensure this kind of thing never happens again.

"It came to me while I was playing fruit ninja," said the PM at a hastily arranged press conference. "I'll leave Letwin and Jumbo Pickles to sort out the details. Byee."

1. A Royal Charter will be introduced, saying no one should introduce any such laws ever again.

2. The Royal Charter will be run by an outsourced, independent, private company with a proven track record of incompetence.

3. Lunch.

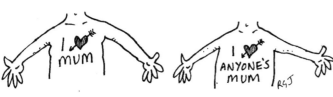

Old-fashioned Tattoo　　　　**Harry Styles' Tattoo**

SPOT THE DIFFERENCE

2010

Osborne blames Labour for wrecking the economy by encouraging a housing bubble

2013

Osborne announces plan to save the economy by creating a housing bubble

---

Nursery Times

.... Friday, Once-upon-a-time ....

APPRENTICE STAR TAKES EMPLOYER TO TRIBUNAL

By Our Legal Staff, **Clive 'Old King' Coleman**

A TALENTED apprentice who won a coveted job working for Sir Alan Sorcerer, began his case today for constrictive dismissal, accusing his employer of treating him like an "overpaid lackey".

The apprentice, a Mr Michael Mouse, believed he had been taken on as a high-level entrepreneurial assistant to run Sir Alan's magic business. In reality, instead of dealing with high-profile wizarding meetings, the apprentice found himself cleaning out the cellar with a mop and broom.

However, Sir Alan dismissed the claims as "pure fantasia". He told the court, "Mickey was fucking useless. I got back one day and the whole cellar was full of water and mops and brooms dancing about to some poncey music. I never really rated Mickey, I only gave the job to a mouse in order to get some publicity."

The absurd cartoon figure admitted telling the mouse "You're fired", but insisted, "he had to go, it was time for a new broom." The case continues.

"...of course, burial at sea can have its drawbacks"

"The check-in desk is over there, this is the chicken desk"

GERMANS SEND MESSAGE TO EUROZONE

A tax is ze best form of defence!

How They Are Related

Prince Harry

Troilus
|
Harald Hardrada
|
Harald Hardrinka
|
King Harry the First
|
Prince Harry the Unclothed
|
Harry Potter
|
Prince Johann Hari
|
The Harry Bikers
|
Harry Krishna
|
Harry Redknapp
|
Harry Redbull
|
Harry Winswar

Cressida Bonas

Cressida
|
Lady Curzon Cinema
|
Lady Curzon Mayfair
|
Lady Curzon Chelsy Davy
|
Lady Curzon Fulham Road now Lady Cineworld
|
Lady Anstruther-Cough-Calpol
|
Lady Amstrad-Sugarfree-Calpol
|
Bono
|
Yasmin le Bonas
|
Lady RBS-Bonas
|
Cressida Sandwich
|
Cressida Bonkas

How the BBC caught the mood of the nation

Presenter: It has just been announced that Baroness Thatcher, the most divisive prime minister of modern times, has died in an expensive hotel in the West End of London. The news had been greeted by many people across the nation with spontaneous street parties, bonfires and choruses of "I'm glad she is dead – who was she again?"

First, however, we can bring you reactions to the news from some of the leading political figures of the Thatcher era.

Gerry Adams: All I can say is that it is a great pity she died in the Ritz Hotel rather than the one in Brighton where we tried to blow her up.

Presenter *(nodding solemnly)*: A heartfelt tribute there from the man who looked on Lady Thatcher as his chief enemy in the struggle for a united Ireland.

Ken Livingstone: She was a disaster for London. Her abolition of the GLC was no less than a major war crime driven by her relentless hatred of ordinary working people. My only regret is that she wasn't put on trial while she was still alive.

Presenter: A sober, historical perspective there from someone who was in a position to see the damage she wrought at first hand.

Anne Scargill, wife of Life President of the NUM Arthur Scargill: My husband is too overcome with joy to speak on this amazing day, but he has asked me to say on behalf of all the working miners of Britain that they are delighted to know that at last the evil, fascist dictator is burning in hell for all the thousands of people she wiped out, after she had turned Britain into a police state.

(Film of thousands of armed policemen beating up miners in 1984)

Presenter: Chilling footage there of the scenes of violence and terror which marked out the Thatcher years. And to provide a uniquely independent view on those terrible times, we have Mrs Thatcher's longtime adversary in the House of Commons, Lord Kinnock.

Lord Kinnock: All I can say about Mrs Thatcher is that she was a total, utter and utterly total disaster as prime minister of this country. To put it another way, Mrs Thatcher was an utter, total and totally utter disaster as prime minister of Britain. Which leads to only one conclusion. Mrs Totally was an utter thatcher as prime Margaret or whatever. I've had a few in the bar to celebrate this utterly and totally joyful day in the long history of our country... Er... the only thing more utterly, totally and utterly totally disastrous for Britain than Mrs Thatcher as prime minister would have been the only alternative on offer at the time, namely, er, hang on, I know what you're thinking, no, let me finish, or rather don't *(continues for 94 hours)*

Presenter But, of course, it wasn't just here in Britain that Thatcher was so controversial, as we hear from the

President of Argentina, Mrs Cristina de Kirchner.

Mrs de Kirchner: The entire world was rightly horrified and outraged in 1982 when the fascist junta, led by Thatcher, invaded Argentine soil by sending a brutal army of occupation to subjugate the Malvinas. I and all patriotic Argentinians can only say, "Rejoice, rejoice" that this imperialist warmonger is dead.

Presenter: That's the international view of Mrs Thatcher from one respected foreign statesman. You can see other comments about her on the BBC website, from other world leaders such as Prime Minister Ahmadinejad of Iran, Kim Jong-Un of North Korea, President Assad of Syria and Tony Blair.

But Mrs Thatcher does have her supporters, who like to claim that her influence on Britain's economy was not entirely destructive.

(Shot of industrial wasteland, half-demolished factories and abandoned shipyards)

But one economic expert who disagrees with this is Will Hutton, Master of Rusbridger College, Oxford.

Hutton: Thatcher was, you know, I mean, personally responsible for, you know, wiping out the whole of British manufacturing in the 1980s, to replace it with a financial sector that was allowed to run totally out of control, thus, you know, bringing about the banking crash and the collapse of Thatcherite capitalism a mere 18 years after she left office, which will be looked on by historians as her true legacy, as carried on by, er, you know, the Labour government, er...

(At this point, viewers turn over to Channel 4 to see Jon Snow interviewing himself about all the times he'd interviewed Mrs Thatcher when she was prime minister. They immediately turn back to the BBC)

Another presenter: ...and with the news that Mrs Thatcher has died, we now talk to some of those men who were her closest colleagues during the years when she exercised supreme power.

(We see a series of clips showing rather sad, elderly men reminiscing about how much they hated working with Mrs Thatcher in the 1980s)

James Prior: The thing I most remember

is that she was frightfully rude to everybody. Particularly poor old Geoffrey. She was always pointing out how useless and wet we all were, particularly Geoffrey. It was jolly unfair and there was nothing that we could do about it.

Geoffrey Howe: Well, one doesn't want to speak ill of the dead, but she really was frightful. And wrong about everything. And she was jolly rude to me. In the end, I was forced to do the only decent thing by stabbing her in the back with a broken cricket bat.

(Shot of Mrs Thatcher weeping in the back of a car leaving Downing Street, played in slow-motion on a loop)

Presenter: Perhaps Lord Howe could claim to have saved the country by his decisive action on that day.

Douglas Hurd: Margaret's one real fault was that she was insufferably rude to us all. She treated us as if we were pretty wet and useless, but she did have her strengths and...

Presenter: I'm afraid I'm going to have to cut you off there. And it is not just old people who couldn't bear Mrs Thatcher. Young people hate her as well, and as a representative of all young people in Britain, we have Cheryl Spart, 19, who is Co-Chair of the Socialist Social Media Against Thatcher Street Party Collective Alliance.

Cheryl: The whole of my life me and my contemporaries have been condemned to live in a Britain dominated on every side by the toxic legacy of Thatcherism... er... even though we weren't alive when she was quite rightly overthrown by the working classes when they finally mobilised in the historic Toxteth and Brixton Poll Tax riots of 1989, when Market Thatcher's attempt to privatise NHS free milk as part of her plan to sell off all Britain's coal mines to provide council houses for yuppie bankers... er... frankly this evil witch is responsible for everything that has gone wrong with Britain, eg global warming, the war in Afghanistan, University tuition fees which are perhaps the greatest single *(cont. p. 94)*

(Millions of viewers switch over at this point with a huge sigh of relief to Broadchurch on ITV)

"What do you mean, you'll miss her?"

theguardian

Margaret Thatcher

Hahahahaha

The death of a former Prime Minister is not the time for childish gloating, but rather for sober contemplation about the old bag's legacy. It would be far too easy merely to revel in the demise of a fellow human being, however different one's outlook, and run editorials saying "Hahahahaha!"

However, even those of us on the left must recognise that the evil old witch had some good points, occasionally got it right, the cow, and that any considered analysis of her eleven years of tyranny would have to concede that, despite being a fascist mass-murderer who would gladly have danced on Nelson Mandela's grave, there were elements in her legislative programme that history will grudgingly judge to have been hahahahaha, she's dead, tramp down the dirt, ding dong the Guardian's nearly dead.

Sun Poll

Who is the greatest woman in history?

● *You decide by putting your tick in the appropriate box*

☐ **Mrs Thatcher**	☒ Princess Diana
☒ Queen Boadicea	☒ Eve
☒ Queen Elizabeth I	☒ Rebekah Brooks
☒ Queen Victoria	☒ Winston Churchill

Send your entries now to the independent polling organisation Youfix, c/o The Sun, Wapping, and we will announce the winner of the Mrs Thatcher Greatest Woman in History Poll in yesterday's paper

---

DAILY ✠ EXPRESS
THE WORLD'S GREATEST NEWSPAPER   FRIDAY, APRIL 19, 2013

WAS THATCHER MURDERED AFTER NIGHT IN RITZ?

By Our Conspiracy Staff
Lady Die

There were growing suspicions last night that the death of Lady Thatcher was not after all due to old age as the police had originally thought.

According to one top forensic expert (Mohammed Al Fayed), "It was murder by the fuggin' Duke of Edinburgh."

He confirmed, "There was a white Fiat Uno seen speeding down the corridor away from the scene.

"The Royals and MI6 were desperate to stop her marrying me and becoming Queen," he foamed and *(cont. p. 94)*

🦅 | THE INDEPENDENT

WAS THATCHER POISONED BY PUTIN? *By Our Crime Correspondent* Libby Dev

She died alone in a London hotel in circumstances that bear all the hallmarks of a KGB hit.

Police are believed to be searching the Ritz for traces of plutonium, although the sinister Russian dictator Vladimir Putin has officially declined to comment on accusations that he personally ordered a hitman to "deal with" the notorious cold warrior and *(cont. p. 94)*

Daily ✠ Maggie
FRIDAY, APRIL 19, 2013

CALLS FOR THATCHER TO BE MADE A SAINT

By Our Entire Staff **Paul Dacre**

Baroness Thatcher was not only the greatest prime minister Britain has ever known and the greatest international statesman of the 20th century. She was also the most wonderful and perfect woman who has ever lived. And now it is time that she was properly recognised by the nation she saved from poverty, servitude, plague, famine and the European Union.

■ We at the Mail were the first to demand that Lady Thatcher should be given a full State Funeral. The Queen has now complied with the wishes of millions of Mail readers, and the ceremony will be a State Funeral in all but name.

■ It was the Mail which demanded that a statue of Baroness Thatcher should be erected on the vacant plinth in Trafalgar Square. But we now believe that, in memory of her own famous victories in Europe, an iron statue of a giant handbag should replace that of Admiral Nelson on top of his famous column.

And, while we're about it, we also demand the following:

● The Falklands should be renamed the Thatcher Islands.

● A portrait of the woman who saved Britain's economy should be carried in perpetuity on the £20 note.

● Heathrow Airport should be renamed London Thatcher Airport (or Thatchrow for short) in honour of the woman who privatised British Airways.

● Our new Archbishop of Canterbury, Justin Welby, should make her the first saint to be made by the Church of England. She should be known appropriately as St Margaret of Assisi and her Saint's Day should be celebrated with a bank holiday on 8 April, the date of her martyrdom at the hands of bile-filled left-wing mobs who celebrated her death by sending each other sickening tweets that are too vile for anyone to have to read.

● And, finally, could there be any finer way to mark the passing of the most saintly woman who has ever walked this earth than to close down the institution which for thirty years has worked night and day to vilify everything she did and to undermine her legacy and which is even now dancing on her grave by refusing to play the disgusting protest song "Ding Dong! The Witch Is Dead"? We refer, of course, to the BBC, which should from now on show only a black screen for the rest of time.

On other pages

● *Those sickening, vile tweets that no one should have to read in full* **94**

NO,NO,NO YOU'RE DOING IT WRONG!

THIS WEEK

CHARLES MOORE

As Lady Thatcher's official biographer, what can you tell us about the part spoons played in her long life?

Margaret Thatcher often spoke to me about spoons. They were a subject of continual interest for her.

Can you explain that?

I think it went back to her formative years at Grantham. Her father, Alderman Roberts, would have encouraged her to do things the right way – when it came to laying the table, for example. The spoons had to be put in the right place and they had to be the right sort – soup or dessert. It was a valuable lesson.

Was that something that stayed with her in later years?

Indeed it was. There was a famous incident when she ticked off a maidservant for giving General Pinochet the wrong sort of teaspoon when she invited him to Chester Square for tea and scones.

Was she concerned about Britain's reputation as a leading world manufacturer of spoons?

Certainly. I have been shown a memo sent to her by the then Chancellor, Geoffrey Howe, with details of his budget plans. She had written "NO VAT ON SPOONS!" with a red felt-tip pen all over it.

Did anything amusing ever happen to her in connection with a spoon?

Ha ha ha. You'll have to read my book to find out, won't you? Ha ha ha.

NEXT WEEK: *Tiger Woods, "Me And My Woods (And My Tiger)"*

Nursery Times
and the
Nursery Sunday Times
(Proprietor: **The Wizened of Oz, R. Murdoch**)

TRIBUTES POUR IN TO WICKED WITCH

STATE FUNERAL TO PROCESS DOWN YELLOW BRICK ROAD

By Our Hagiography Staff, **William Hagiography**

FOLLOWING the sad death of the Wicked Witch who passed away after a whirlwind illness last week, the Land of Oz was united in its grief for the late lamented witch.

Tributes poured in from across the country – apart from a few anarchist munchkins who danced around singing a disrespectful song to celebrate her death.

We at the Nursery Times are not going to dignify this song by repeating it, but needless to say the left-wing BBC (Bedtime Broadcasting Company) has disgracefully allowed "Ding Dong the Witch is Dead" to appear on its "Top of the Pop Your Clogs Show".

However, one of the witch's flying monkeys, Mr B. Ingham, played down the effect of the munchkin protest and said, "The demonstrations were very small, as indeed are the munchkins. These are just little people and it's what you would expect of them."

Said top political expert the Wizened of Oz, "The Wicked Witch transformed Oz from the grim black and white world it once was to the gaudy technicolour fantasy land it is today.

"We all owe her a huge debt of gratitude, especially me, and anyone who says she was wicked is either cowardly, heartless or brainless – or a wet girl like Dorothy."

The Wizened of Oz is 94.

The Mrs Thatcher I Never Knew

By Our Commemorative Staff Eve Ryone

I WAS privileged to have never known Mrs Thatcher personally and therefore have been given a unique insight into what she wasn't really like.

Publicly, she was a tough, forceful woman who wanted to get her own way. In private, she might well have been kind, compassionate and considerate to all, but I have no idea.

I will never forget the time I didn't meet her. It was in Grimsditch on a cold February morning in 1979. The news went round town, "Mrs Thatcher isn't here. She's in Guildford".

And, amazingly, aged 27, and on my first job as a cub reporter on the trade magazine *Fish and Fishmen*, I was only 94 miles away in Mucklethorpe.

But for a cruel twist of fate I might have met Mrs Thatcher that day and, indeed, I didn't meet her on many subsequent occasions. Each time I was touched by how different she was from how she might have been had I actually met her.

One thing, however, is for sure. I am not going to miss the chance to make some money out of her passing. It's what she would have wanted.

© *All hacks, April 2013.*

DING DONG!

How dare you be so disrespectful!

POETRY CORNER

In Memoriam Baroness Thatcher of Kesteven, 1925-2013

So. Farewell
Then
Baroness Thatcher.

Your supporters
Say you made
Britain what
It is today.

So do your
Critics.

They claim
You will go
To Hell.

But Keith's mum
Says, "The lady
Is not for
Burning".

E.J. Thribbute (17½)

THATCHER LEGACY

She's certainly left her Mark

"Well, at least we got closure..."

"As most of us know, Bill was one of the best prop makers in the film industry"

HEIR OF SORROWS
Another Short Story Special
by Dame Sylvie Krin, author of
Duchess of Hearts & *You're Never Too Old*

THE STORY SO FAR: Prince Charles has twice suffered disappointment after misunderstanding snatches of news bulletins on the wireless whilst taking his bath. The abdication of the Queen of the Netherlands and the retirement of the Pope as leader of his church both raised Charles' expectations, only for him to see them cruelly dashed. Now read on...

CHARLES could feel himself unwinding in the fragrant embrace of the steamy water infused with the bubbling essences of Duchy Original Organic Foot 'n' Mouth Bath Balm. Sir Alan Fitztightly, trusted courtier and Royal Toothpaste Squeezer Poursuivant, sashayed into the room carrying a new DAB Statute Radio.

"Where shall I put this?" asked Sir Alan, adding tartly, "...as dear old Backstairs Billy used to say to all the new footmen when he..."

"Just put it on the side, thank you very much, Sir Alan," said Charles. "And can we have that nice Eddie Marr on Start the PM?"

"Very good, Sire." Sir Alan turned on the set and backed out of the room, discreetly leaving Charles to relax as the reassuring sounds of Radio Four filled the air. That was better... now what were they discussing?... Some constitutional thingie? And wasn't that the John Prescott chap...? He could hear the distinctive northern voice of the former Deputy Leader of the Leader party...

"...which is why the immediate resignating of Her Majesty the Queen in abdicatedness is necessitary forthwithstanding and..."

Charles sprang from the bath in one bound and, stopping only to cover his modesty with a Royal Family Guy Flannel (a gift from Prince Harry after his last trip to Las Vegas), he sped semi-naked down the corridor *(cont. p. 94)*

FARAGE LATEST

I'm ten pints ahead in the polls

WE REVEAL THE SCANDALOUS SECRET OF BRITAIN'S SECRET COURTS

by Our Secret Courts Staff
(whose names cannot be given for legal reasons)

IF the people of Britain knew what travesties of justice take place behind the closed doors of our fast-expanding secret court system, they would be shocked, horrified and outraged.

But, scandalously, they are not allowed to know what goes on because the judges have ruled that it is too secret for any of it to be revealed to the public.

That is why today this newspaper has decided to take on this iniquitous and semi-totalitarian reign of secret terror head on, and to blow apart the wall of silence which the court system has for too long erected around itself to conceal its shameful workings from public view.

That is why we are today reporting for the first time the horrifying case of ▓▓▓▓▓▓ and ▓▓▓▓▓▓ council. This case was brought in ▓▓▓▓ before Mr Justice ▓▓▓▓▓, who ordered that ▓▓▓▓▓ should be ▓▓▓▓▓, with the tragic result that ▓▓▓▓

Unfortunately, for legal reasons, the rest of this heroic attempt to challenge the deeply disturbing stranglehold of Britain's secret courts has had to be removed, following an injunction issued yesterday by Lord Justice ▓▓▓▓▓, the exact terms of which we are forbidden to report, as we are unable to reveal the names of the authors of this article who are now in prison for reasons which we cannot disclose.

© *All newspapers.*

Alex Salmond's Shopping List for Scottish Independence

1 We are prepared to retain Queen Elizabeth II as sovereign of the new independent Scotland, so long as she changes her name to James VIII.

2 We are prepared to retain the Pound Sterling as the currency of the new independent Scotland, so long as no one points out that until last year I was very keen that we should join the Euro.

3 We are prepared to retain the name Scotland as the title of the new independent Scotland until such time as the Scottish people shall be allowed to choose by referendum one of the following alternatives:

i) Braveheartia
ii) Salmondia
iii) Bankruptia.

(That's enough. Ed.)

"Tomorrow's chip paper"

ROBERT THOMPSON

Film highlights
Leveson Actually

Classic court-room rom-com, in which dashing floppy-haired barrister Hugh Grant QC (played by an on-form David Sherborne) falls for pretty junior counsel, the mysterious "woman on the left", Martine McCutcheon (played by perky Carine Patry Hoskins). Will their tangled personal lives get in the way of press freedom, or will love triumph?

Watch out for the hysterical set-piece on the Greek island of Nookios, where they meet for a passionate discussion about whether or not they should have a relationship, though after the inquiry obviously, so as not to give the impression of a conflict of interest.

Scene-stealing performance by Lord Leveson as the hapless judge Mr Justice Bill Nighy, as he looks embarrassed and claims he had no idea what was going on – much like Mr Murdoch, hilariously played in previous scenes by Rowan Atkinson. *(Is this right? Ed.)*

***EYE RATING:** Phwoar stars*

The Adventures of Mr Milibean
Fountain & Jamieson

IT'S OBVIOUS I HAD MANY DISAGREEMENTS WITH THE EX-PRIME MINISTER...

...THE CALLOUSNESS, THE UNFETTERED CAPITALISM, THE RIGHT WING POSTURING...

BUT I THINK IT'S IMPORTANT TO MARK THE DEATH OF SUCH A HUGE FIGURE WHO LED THIS COUNTRY...

DAILY BLAB
BLAIR RIPS INTO MILIBEAN

THE SOONER THE BETTER!

HENRY DAVIES

DIARY

MICK AND KEITH REMEMBER

KEITH: It was like, totaw madness.

MICK: Yeah. Totaw maaaadness. What we talkin' about?

KEITH: Y'know. The totaw madness.

MICK: Righ! Yeah! Totaw maaaadness. But TOTAL!

KEITH: Totaw wha?

MICK: Maaadness. Totaw fuckin' maaadness!

KEITH: Yeah, totaw madness.

MICK: Yeah. It was like, totaw maaaaadness.

✳✳✳

MICK: First chick I ever shagged? Yeah, righ. Wooh! Righ! You gomme there!

KEITH: Grace.

MICK: Wha? Grace Slick? You never shagged her!

KEITH: Nah. Gracie Fields. Round the back of the wodgermicallit.

MICK: Camper van?

KEITH: Thassit. Camper van. While you was inside with Ruth?

MICK: Ruth? Ruth? Nah! Remind me?

KEITH: Ruth, Lady Fermoy. Jeez! Talk about Lady in Waiting! Not much waiting when she was around, hur, hur!

MICK: Totaw madness!

✳✳✳

MICK: Keith and me, we firs met somewhere – where was it. Keith?

KEITH: In the stree. We met in the stree. You member!

MICK: Yeah, in the stree! Dr Livingstone, I presume! Righ!!!

KEITH: Nah, I don' member Dr Livingstone? Who the fucks Dr Livingstone when hes at home?

MICK: He wasn' at home. That's the whole fuckin' point of Dr Livingstone, he wasn' at home. He was abraw. Anyway, so Keith and me, first time we met, it was in the stree.

KEITH: Or it may of bin indoors.

MICK: Thassit. Indoors! It was indoors! Keith and me, first time we met, it was indoors! Classic!

KEITH: Not OUTdoors, but INdoors! There's a fuck of a difference, Mick. Outdoors is out, an' indoors is in.

MICK: Well, it was either outdoors or indoors. Or, to put it another way, indoors or outdoors. The main thing was we met.

KEITH: Thas if we DID ever meet. I can't member.

MICK: 'Course we fuckin' met, Keith. `If we hadn' met, we wouldn't be, like, here today…

KEITH: We're talkin bow years ago. Litree years and years ago.

MICK: Fifty years ago!

KEITH: You're kiddin'.

MICK: Thas the whole fuckin' poin', Keith! Thas wha' we're celebraaaatin'!

KEITH: Fifty years. Fifty fuckin' years!

MICK: Fifty fuckin' years of like totaw fuckin' maaaadness! Bring it on, maaan!

✳✳✳

MICK: We've always bin anti-establishmen'.

KEITH: Yeah, we've always really hated the anti-establishmen'.

MICK: Nah, Keith – we're anti-establishmen'. That means we don' hate the anti-establishmen', we hate the establishmen'.

KEITH: Swotter sed. Hey, man, I'm coo.

✳✳✳

KEITH: Firs time we were on Tobbaverpobz. When was the firs time we were on Tobbaverpobz? Was it wiv the chick in the tartan skirt. Wossername? You know, she sang "You'll take the fuckin' high road and I'll take the fuckin' wodever road, and we'll be somewhere like cool in the morning."

MICK: Andy Stewart? He wasn't a chick, he was a bloke, Keith, a Scottish bloke in a kilt.

KEITH: Who gives a fuck, maaan? She was a naughty little lady, bless her heart. Made an old man very happy, hur hur hur.

✳✳✳

MICK: So, history-wise, there was Brian –

KEITH: Wodever happened to him?

MICK: Dead.

KEITH: Shame. Rest in wodever.

MICK: Then there was Mick –

KEITH: Thought you was Mick.

MICK: Yeah, I'm Mick but there was another Mick too.

KEITH: Two Micks. Faaaar out. Two Micks. That really does me head in. Wappened tim then? 'e die too?

MICK: Nah, jus left.

KEITH: Same difference, hur hur hur.

MICK: Then came Ronnie.

KEITH: Ronnie? Who the fuck? Remind me.

MICK: Y'know – Woody.

KEITH: Thought you said 'e was called Ronnie.

MICK: Ronnie Woody. Spiky hair. Guitar.

KEITH: Always wondered who 'e was. 'Bout time someone told me. Had some good times together, man.

MICK: Yeah, memories!

KEITH: Yeah, righ. But wha' memories? Remind me.

As told to C R A I G   B R O W N

Fallen angels

"When I said check on him at twenty-fifteen I meant THE TIME, not THE YEAR!"

"Mrs Gridlington doesn't like being referred to as 'duck' or 'dearie'... so I just call her 'the old bag who complains'!"

"Well, he may be DEAD, but according to our 'client satisfaction survey', he's pretty happy about it!"

"Whistleblowers don't need to fear PERSECUTION, just ask Dr Wainscott here!"

QUEEN'S SPEECH: AUSTERITY BITES

She's wearing the same hat as last year

---

theguardian

When will we ever learn?

It is with a heavy heart that we see that Boston bomb suspects Dzhokhar and Tamerlan Tsarnaev have already been labelled as Muslim terrorists just because they've carried out a terror attack and were Muslims.

"Perhaps if right-wingers weren't so quick to label Muslims who carry out terror attacks as Muslim terrorists, fewer young men would become radicalised and end up being labelled as Muslim terrorists simply because they've carried out a terror attack that kills innocent (cont. p. 94.)

NEWS IN BRIEF

Internet users 'criticise police'

Amateur detectives on social media sites such as Twitter and Reddit have criticised Boston police for hunting down and finding the actual culprits who carried out the Boston marathon bombing.

"Using our skills honed from years of watching Scooby Doo, it took just minutes for us to identify an innocent man online and accuse him of being a terrorist," said one Reddit user.

"For the police to ignore this and instead actually investigate and track down the real perpetrators shows they do not understand the internet age in which we live.

"They should be joining our internet vigilante mob, burning down the homes of innocent people, rather than wasting time and resources catching bombers."

Lessons to learn

The frenzy of unsubstantiated rumours on the internet and twenty-four hour news channels in the wake of the Boston Bombing has led to calls for a type of printed pamphlet to be invented that would sift through this welter of disinformation and discover the actual facts of the case.

"We could perhaps call this 'printed pamphlet' a NEWS-PAPER," said one internet user. "This NEWS-PAPER would employ trained staff to give perspective and analysis to the tragic events."

The idea was quickly rejected by everyone online as hopelessly old fashioned, saying provided they got their information instantly, they simply didn't care how inaccurate it was.

OPERATION YEWTREE

THE FINGER OF SUSPICION

"He's two and he isn't talking, but the doctor said not to be concerned"

THOSE UKIP POLICIES IN FULL

1. Smoking to be allowed in pubs.
2. Waxed jackets to be made mandatory.
3. Chaps not obliged to help with the washing up.
4. VAT on beards.
5. Massive investment in golf club construction.
6. Driving gloves to be worn in cars at all times.
7. Bring back Robertson's Golly on marmalade jars.
8. Police permitted to give young offenders a clip round the ear.
9. Black and white TV to return.
10. Johnny foreigner to get marching orders... whoops.

Korean Leaders – A Guide

South Korea	North Korea

Psy	**Psycho**
Crazy horse-riding funnyman happy to rock the world with one smash-hit	Crazy horse-riding funnyman happy to rock the world with one smash-hit

Yes it's MADMAN style!

UKIP 'Momentum now unstoppable'

UKIP was celebrating yet more stunning election results in the wake of not winning the Eastleigh by-election with it triumphantly not winning a by-election in South Shields or taking control of any English council.

"Should these phenomenal results be replicated at the General Election, it would see us sweeping to victory with no seats at Westminster and UKIP controlling zero councils across the UK," a jubilant Nigel Farage told supporters as he held his pint glass triumphantly aloft.

"At which point Her Majesty would have no choice but to ask us to form the new Government."

Those local election results in full

(cont. from p. 1)

East Wessex County Council

Horsebrassington Ward

Patsy Windfarm *(Green)* 2

Nick Sandal *(Lib Dem)* 1

Tim Heathcoat Amory *(Conservative)* 45

Fred Heathcoat Amory *(Labour)* 3

Godfrey Golfclub *(Monster Raving UKIP Party)* 3,412

UKIP gain from Con.

Turnout 8.3 percent

(That's quite enough county election results. Ed.)

"Witchcraft causing our crops to fail?! D'you take us for simple, half-witted bumpkins? Obviously, the true reason is the combination of Britain's EU membership and gay marriage"

Benefits policies 'not working' shock

MR Iain Duncan Smith admitted last night that a lot of his policies were not actually working, even though he said they were "perfectly capable of doing so".

He told the House of Commons, "It's my job to get these policies working. To be honest, most of them are just lazy and can't be bothered to do what they are supposed to."

He continued, "Only by cutting their funding will these policies have the incentive to work, especially those which are clearly unfit to achieve anything at all."

(Rotters)

Jamie Oliver's Recipe Of The Day

Nutty Fruitcake

1. Get loadsa luvly nuts.
2. Add some more nuts.
3. Stir it up a bit.
4. Bish bosh.
5. Half bake for 10 minutes.
6. Join UKIP.

One seriously nutty fruitcake – sorted! Luvly Jubbly!

© Jamie 2013

Sir Charles Moore

The official biographer to Baroness Thatcher of Kesteven addresses the vexed issue of whether Maggie was a bit of a goer at Oxford

IT WAS then that the young Margaret turned her attention to the dashing former fighter pilot, Squadron Leader 'Squiffy' Squiffington, who was studying Molecular Biology at Brownnose College. Squiffy took the young Margaret Hilda Roberts to the Bore's Hill Conservative Party Dinner and Dance and the two later went back to his rooms in Old Grope Quad. Squiffington recalls a "high degree of physical amorosity" although Margaret's letter to her sister at the time merely refers to her inamorato as a "flirty fellow Tory".

My own view, as a serious historian, based on 979 in-depth interviews with all the key participants over the last ten years, is that, Crikey! Ding dong!, she was all over him, positively gagging for it! And that night, as his experienced hands ripped the bodice from her eager young *(cont. p. 994)*

© Margaret Thatcher: "The page is for turning" by Sir Charles Phwoarrr.

The Eye's Controversial New Columnist

When he's tired and emotional, it's not a metaphor

This week I am very angry at suggestions that a lot of babies are going to turn out to be Boris Johnson's love children. I categorically deny that this is the case.

In other, completely unrelated news, I have spent a very constructive week in nursery, creating a Lego island in the corner of the paddling pool so I can land my Fisher-Price planes, and have successfully introduced a 'pay as you amble' scheme for the tricycles in the playground.

This more than made up for my momentary embarrassment on Monday when I was suspended in the air for several minutes when my baby bouncer malfunctioned! I was slightly alarmed when I caught my reflection in my shiny new mobile and saw this huge mop of blond (cont. p. 94)

"And this is where I met your mum"

An Apology

IN RECENT weeks, in common with all other newspapers, we have run a great many articles describing Sir Alex Ferguson, the retiring manager of Manchester United Football Club, as an almost superhuman figure, the greatest leader of men this country has known since Winston Churchill and undoubtedly "the greatest living Briton".

We now realise, with the retirement of Sir David Beckham from professional football, that our tributes to Sir Alex were ridiculously hyperbolic and grotesquely over-inflated. We now realise that it is Sir David who is an almost superhuman figure, the greatest leader of men this country has known since Winston Churchill and undoubtedly the greatest loving Briton *(shurely shome mishtake?)*.

We apologise for any confusion that may have been caused by this error and look forward to repeating it all over again when it comes to the retirement of Sir Harold Redknapp or the reappointment of Señor José Mourinho as manager of Oligarski FC. *(That's enough football. Ed.)*

the PREMIERSH*TS

PAUL WOOS

FERGIE'S RETIREMENT — THE PLAYERS' VERDICT...

CANTONA

WHEN THE SEAGULLS FOLLOW THE HAIRDRYER...

KEANE

RED MIST

☆*©**

VAN NISTELROOY

HE LIKES A GOOD NAG

GIGGS

I LOVE HIM LIKE A BROTHER'S WIFE

BECKHAM

FERGIE, YEH BLAH, BLAH...

JUST MAKE SURE YOU GET A GOOD SHOT OF MY PANTS

POETRY CORNER

Lines on the retirement of Sir Alex Ferguson

So. Farewell
Then, Sir Alex.

Yes. You were
Britain's most successful
Football manager.

It was never a penalty.
That was your catch phrase.

It was a definite penalty
That was another.

E.J. aThribb (17 points clear at
top of the Premiership)

DIARY

THE LATE MICHAEL WINNER

"What sort of rubbish place do you call this, then?" I asked. A servile underling told me it was heaven.

I took one look. What a shambles! Clouds everywhere, blokes with unkempt beards, choirs caterwauling, the lot. And who the bloody hell ordered all those ghastly harps?

"If this is heaven," I replied, "I demand to see the manager!"

I'll tell you the worst thing of all. The so-called Pearly Gates. Frankly, I've seen classier pearls hanging round the neck of a two-dollar tart. Plus they could do with a decent polish. All very second-rate.

And who in their right mind wants pearls splashed all over a gate anyway?

Gates are for opening and shutting. You don't want them mucked around.

A surly apparatchik calling himself St Peter strides over. Says he's the manager. Bit of a bossy-boots. No tie. Beard sprouting any-old-how, most unhygienic. Right know-it-all.

"Name?" he says, looking down at his clipboard.

"Don't you know who I am?" I respond. "How very dare you! I've never been treated like this in my life!"

At this point, the choir of heavenly angels start their so-called singing. What a racket! "Glo-o-o-oria!" they howl. Totally tuneless. And who is this Gloria anyway? No one I've ever heard of, and I've known all the big stars as very close personal friends. Roger Moore. John Cleese. That one from The Sweeney. The lot.

I politely tell the choir to put a sock in it and shut their gobs. "If I want to strangle a cat, I'll strangle a cat!" I say. It's a classic Winner put-down. Pure gold. But it's lost on them, of course. They just carry on singing. Did no one ever teach them manners? I've never known such disgusting behaviour in all my born days.

I notice that all the men are wearing white smocks. Terrible for stains.

"I wouldn't be seen dead in one, dear," I tell them.

"But you ARE dead, Michael," they reply. Most discourteous. What a revolting bunch.

The self-styled St Peter – how these people love their titles – proves most unreasonable. The man simply doesn't know his place. I inform him in no uncertain terms that I'm absolutely sick to the back teeth with uppity receptionists.

"That's enough of the monkey! Let me speak to the organ-grinder!" I demand. Another classic Winner put-down!

At last I get prompt service. A red-faced man with horns and a tail, carrying an over-large fork, rushes over. He beckons me to follow him downstairs.

"You misunderstand me. I never eat in basements," I respond. "Don't you know who I am?"

He assures me that a huge number of my very dear friends from the movie business are all there, waiting to greet me. "Very well," I say. "Just this once. But you'd better put on a decent show – or there'll be hell to pay"

"We'll be showing you all your films, 24/7, on a spool, for the next 2000 years," he replies, as he leads me down.

As told to CRAIG BROWN

EVERYONE WHO APPEARED ON TV IN THE 70s ARRESTED

by Our Crime Staff **Dawn Swoop**

HUNDREDS of old men – many of them long since dead – were arrested yesterday in a series of police raids the length and breadth of Britain.

Leading Operation Gropebusters was Inspector "Knacker of the Yard". Knacker told a vast crowd of specially invited reporters, "We have now successfully arrested pretty well every famous person who ever appeared on television back in the infamous period known as the 1970s.

"Acting on tip-offs from members of the public, many of whom remember seeing these people on television when they were young, we have rounded up all the nation's favourite presenters and entertainers of that unsavoury era, in the certain knowledge that they must have been up to no good with underage girls, young boys or in some cases probably even household pets.

"My officers," he went on, "are dedicating their efforts 24/7 to watching old comedy programmes, regional news broadcasts and weather forecasts in the hope of identifying some celebrity of that seedy epoch that we haven't yet taken into custody."

When asked how he could justify the deployment of 25,000 officers working full-time on the biggest police operation since World War Two, Inspector Knacker arrested all the reporters on the grounds of aiding and abetting serial paedophilia.

"What a fantastic cause... and it's only three pounds"

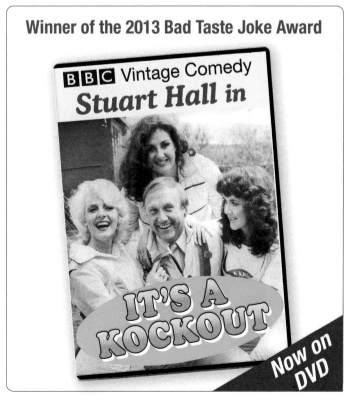
GNOME SPORT
CHELSEA REPLACE MANAGER

OUT

IN

FARAGE APPEALS TO TORY ACTIVISTS

If you object to being called a swivel-eyed loon, join UKIP!

Notes & queries

What is a 'Swivel-Eyed Loon'?

● A 'Swivel-Eyed Loon' is a species of bird, usually found around golf courses. It is noted for its unusual flying patterns, going round and round in circles due to an overly developed right wing. The loon refuses to leave these shores, is extremely aggressive towards migratory birds, protecting its territory with a shrill shriek as well as its trademark huffing and puffing. The swivel eyes allow the loon to ignore what's going on around it, and concentrate on its primary task, which is to drop excrement on its leader from a very great height. Once thought extinct, the swivel-eyed loon is now once again flourishing in the grass-roots-lands of the Home Counties.
The Reverend T. Twitcher

● The good Reverend is sadly talking nonsense, the phrase 'Swivel-Eyed Loons' was first applied in the Teapot Rising of 1874 by Major General P.G. Tipps to describe Chinese rebel soldiers from Kowloon, high on Lapsang Souchong, who were besieging the British Garrison at Fort Twai-Ning. The General was later relieved of his command by Earl Grey.
Professor Niall Ferguson

● May I just pick up on Mrs Kardashian's claim that the Rooney's child 'Klay' was named after the boxer Kassius Klay, who, unlike his famous namesake, never became world champion, but did set up a mildly successful gym in Krosby, Merseyside? This is fanciful nonsense. Klay comes from the Greek 'Klaeon', meaning the child of the wife and or girlfriend of the Philosopher King. See Euripides' famous tragedy 'Klaeon and the Red Card'. Wayne Rooney, by choosing the name, has proved that far from being just a simple striker, capable of playing in the hole behind Van Persie, he is a thoughtful and well-read classicist, steeped in the traditions of Plato's Republic and Hello.
Professor Alex Ferguson

Answers please:
What is 'summer'?
How do you grow a Yew Tree?
What's so great about the Gatsby?

"Do you think, perhaps, you are really angry at yourself?"

How They Are Related
UN Power Couple

William Hague	Angelina Jolie
Pitt the Younger	Brad Pitt
Pitt the Elder	Angel Gabriel
Hague the Younger	Angel Islington
Hague the Middle-Aged	Angelina Merkel
Hague the Elder	Brangelina
Field Marshal Haig	Brangella Lawson
Just William	Joely Richardson
Prince William of Orange	Jolene Jolene Joleeeeeeene
will.i.am Hague	Dom Jolie
William Hague-International-criminalcourt	**Angelina Jolie-goodfellow**

DON'T GIVE THEM THE OXYGEN OF PUBLICITY!

Inside: Hundreds of graphic pictures, videos, interviews, comments, editorials etc.

94-PAGE WOOLWICH TERROR SPECIAL

NHS CHIEF NICHOLSON RESIGNS

We're losing him

Hooray!

Hooray!

Hooray!

HOME OFFICE

ALL OUR TERRORISM IS LOCALLY SOURCED

RSJ

CAMERON VOWS TO END RADICALISATION

DAVID CAMERON has made a stirring speech in the House of Commons urging the people of Britain to build robust structures to reject extremism.

"Unless we drain this vile marsh of intolerance, these people are going to grow up more and more poisoned by their sick ideology, which will prompt them to ever more violent and disruptive activities," the Prime Minister said.

"These will include objections to gay marriage, leaving Europe, bringing back fox hunting and smoking in pubs, not to mention kicking me out of office immediately, which is precisely what makes them so very dangerous".

The Prime Minister's taskforce will disrupt extremist groups (also known as "Local Conservative Associations") by infiltrating them, intercepting their communications, and, in extreme cases, by banning them outright. *(AP)*

Afghan interpreters given visas

by Our Military Staff **Michael Buerqa**

THE Ministry of Defence has at last agreed that its Afghan interpreters should be allowed to escape the danger and violence of Britain's streets and go back to the safety of Afghanistan.

"It's just too dangerous here," said one frightened interpreter. "The place is full of murderous extremists. We're better off taking our chances in Helmand province."

Are you ageing?

Five tell-tale signs

1. You are getting tired of these pointless surveys rehashed in newspapers and which aren't news.

2. You keep saying, "In my day there was proper news in the paper".

3. Er...

4. That's...

5. It.

MY WIFE DOESN'T UNDERSTAND ME

UNSYMPATHETIC, EH?

NO, THAI

WARNER & PEARSON

DESPERATE BUSINESS

JON & MICK / MODERN TOSS

just got rid of my spare room,
who do I see about a rebate?

bloke here wants to know
if he can test drive a bath

That's £4.50 for the sandwich

yeah I don't normally pay for stuff
I'm going to review on my website?

he's concentrating on disabled parking
permits, that's where the money is

this Bond DVD has got someone walking
across the screen halfway through

yeah that's actually me,
d'you want me to sign it?

A Doctor Writes

AS A doctor, I'm often asked, "I'm feeling terrible, can I come and see you in your surgery?".

The simple answer is as follows:

a) You are not allowed to ring me up, you can only contact my surgery via email.

b) It is now 5.25 on a Friday afternoon and I have left the surgery until Monday morning.

c) You should contact the out-of-hours service provided for the NHS by G4S Capita Health on 0870-444-4444 (calls cost £1.89 a minute).

d) If you can't afford this, ring the new NHS Emergency Advice line on 111 and you will be able to listen to a few bars of soothing, therapeutic Pachelbel's Canon repeated for several hours, until you are eventually connected to a friendly "agent" in Hyderabad who will advise you to visit the Accident and Emergency Unit at your nearest NHS hospital that hasn't been closed down.

e) Drive 30 miles to nearest A&E to find that, owing to overwhelming demand and a shortage of trained doctors, you are in a 5-hour queue.

f) By this time, my advice as a GP is that you will probably either feel better or you will be dead.

© A. Doctor 2013.

best of the web

This one is going viral from the respected jfkisstillalive.blog

No one should be taken in by the so-called Oklahoma "tornado" story fed to the gullible MSM by the Pentagon/CIA complex. The pattern of destruction in the photographs of Moore is totally inconsistent with the normal impact footprint of an EF-5 tornado. What we are actually witnessing here is a massive cover-up to hide a catastrophic error by the US military who, on the date in question, were testing out a new super-drone (see atlastthefacts.blogspot.com), which was intended to remove a command and control centre in Aleppo, Syria, but which went disastrously wrong. The flightpath of the drone was tracked by amateur observers (see dronespottersunited.wordpress.com) as making a U-turn over the Atlantic and heading back to Oklahoma, with the results that are now tragically history. Nothing more clearly gives away the transparent fakery of the cover-up than the clumsy Photoshopping of a tornado imposed on the scenes of devastation (see the greatapolloelevenhoax.huffpost.com) that had in fact been caused by a criminal blunder by the USAAF control team in Arizona. But will we see President O'Bomber having the courage and honesty to admit this to the world? I think not!

● See also the excellent 9/11wasciamossaddukeofedinburghplot. fuggingtonpost.com, which has had over 2 billion hits in 24 hours.

PUZZLE CORNER

Rearrange the following letters and see what new words you can find?

U K I P

Answer: BNP, EDL, NF, NBG

LOBBYING SCANDAL GROWS

BUNG!

BUNG!

BUNG!

Oh no, it's Big Bent

PEER CAUGHT ADMITTING 'I'D DO ANYTHING FOR MONEY'

by Our Investigative Staff **Peers Moron**

THE respected peer Lord Lobby of Sleaze (formerly Sir Len Bribe, the MP for Cash-under-Counter, Staffs) has been exposed by an Eye investigative sting as corrupt, greedy and perfectly fit to continue sitting in the House of Lords.

Eye journalists, posing as members of a lobbying company acting on behalf of a solar wind farm project in the Gilbert and Sullivan Islands, approached Lord Sleaze with an offer to pay £2,000 an hour to act as a consultant, and a further £10,000 to ask a question in the House of Lords.

Lord Sleaze was secretly filmed happily accepting the money we offered him and saying, "You won't regret this – I am a great personal friend of every member of both front benches, and I can get you a private meeting with key people such as Oliver Letwin any time."

When we confronted Lord Sleaze last night with the evidence

that he was prepared to take "cash for access", he told us, "I don't see what your problem is. I only did what most MPs and peers do every day. It's how government works in Britain.

"I have years of unstinting service to my country," he added, "and it's time for the country to give me something back."

However, Lord Sleaze refused to discuss the "perfectly innocent question" he tabled in the House of Lords last February, in the course of a debate on gay marriage, which asked, "Does Her Majesty's Government agree with me that the Gilbert and Sullivan Islands are not only ideally suited to act as a venue for same-sex marriages, but also, blessed as they are with abundant sunshine and continuous breezes from the Pacific Ocean, are a perfect location for the building of a huge solar windfarm of the type being proposed by the excellent South Sea Bubble Solar Wind Company?".

NEW FIVER

Bank of England

Never has so much been owed by so many

Five Pounds

"I have nothing to offer but blood, toil, tears and sweat"

MP IN CASH FOR QUESTIONS SCANDAL

By Our Parliamentary Correspondent **Lobby Purves**

An MP has been caught doing the job he's paid to do – to the huge embarrassment of most of his colleagues.

The backbencher was secretly filmed on the Parliament Channel tabling questions on behalf of his constituents in order to improve the quality of their lives. In return, he was given an annual over-the-counter payment of £66,000.

When confronted with his actions the MP said, "I can't believe I've been so stupid. This isn't the kind of behaviour that's expected of an MP.

"I shall resign immediately, and apologise to my fellow Members for so thoughtlessly upholding the standards of the House."

Aztec 'Naughty Step'

GLENDA SLAGG

She's the gal who asks questions for cash!?!! Geddit!?!

■ **JEREMY Irons – What a stupid old Bore-gia!?! Geddit!!? Fancy saying that the innocent gals on Top of the Pops were all goers who were gaggin' for it!? What a disgrace!! That's just wishful thinking on your behalf, Grandad!!? Just cos you played an old perv in "Lolita" doesn't mean it's alright to _be_ one!?! You're not Top of the Popes in my book!?!!**

■ **JEREMY Irons – at last someone has had the guts to point out that all the leggy Lolitas on Top of the Pops (Top of the Popsies, I call it!!?) were right ravers a-wigglin' and a-jigglin' round the studio!?! Good for you, Jeremy. It's a brave man who tells it like it is, particularly when he's played a paedo in the pix!?! You're absolutely Borgeous and definitely my Top of the Popes!?!! Geddit?!?**

■ **MYLEENE Klass – TMI!!! That's too much information, Myleene!!? OK, so you enjoy a nice cup of breast milk in your morning cuppa!? Eurghhh!! We just don't want to know!!? And now you're milking it for all it's worth. What a Klass Act?? NOT!?!!**

■ **MYLEENE pure Klass!!? What could be more charming than the thought of a cosy cuppa with a drop of mama Myleene's mammary magic!?! Mmmm... Cancel that pinta, Mr Milkman!?!**

■ **SO Karl Lagerfeld wants to marry his cat!!? Why not – they'd make the purrfect couple??! One's a highly strung, whiney, scratchy little feline – and so's the other one!?!! Geddit?!? It's a miaowrage made in heaven!!?!**

■ **KARL Lagerfeld and his Moggy Mate!?! It's a miaowrage made in hell!!? Someone's got to stop the poor deluded creature getting hitched – and I don't mean Karl!!?**

■ **KATE Winslet's had another kiddie with yet another fella!!? It's what we call a 3 x 3!?! And why not?!? Lay off Kate, Mr Prudish Pressman??! She's just a modern miss with multiple misters!?!! Geddit?!?**

■ **KATE Winslet – what a slapper!!?**
(You're fired, Ed.)

Byeee!!

Nation celebrates sixty years of Royal dynasty

by **Our Royal Staff** Jenny Flect

Sixty years after the Coronation and still going strong – the Dimbleby family may have had its ups and downs, including marital break-ups and embarrassing relatives, but through it all the serene figure of David Dimbleby has remained constant.

Dimbleby has become a byword for public service and duty, as he travels all around the country in his Landrover asking people, "What do you do?"

And there he was again last week, turning out for yet another state pageant – an official Service of Remembrance for Himself as he ably took the microphone one more time to say in those familiar tones, "And there is the Duke of Lymeswold, carrying the Trouserpress of State, first used by King Edward the Fox in 1927".

But constitutionalists ask whether it is time for David to abdicate and make way for the unpopular heir apparent – the Welsh pretender – Huw Edwards?

No, say the loyalists. Let's keep Dimbleby in his rightful place as King of Broadcasting and Defender of the BBC until such a point as he dies on air.

Others disagree, saying it is time for Dimbleby to step down gracefully, just as his father did before him, and pass on his onerous Royal duties to the next generation – ie, his son *(is this right? Ed.)*

The Eye Says...

God Bless You Dimblema'am! Long may you commentate in the rain!

HOUSE OF LORDS BACKS GAY MARRIAGE

"There's something wrong with my German Shepherd dog..."

THEATRE NEWS

'Book of Moron' opens

ALL of London is talking about the new show "The Book of Moron", the outrageously controversial musical which is guaranteed to have you rolling in the aisles! The show tells the story of a Moron who arrives in a new country, fleeing the ignominy which bedevilled his past. The born-again Moron sees the light during a chance encounter with a mirror, and determines to make everyone worship himself. Featuring songs like "You and Me (But Mostly Me)", "Making It Up Again" and "All American Prophet", the show is clearly designed to depict the average Moron (Piers) as a figure of fun.

Eye rating: z-z-z-z-z-z

iPhony

APPLE, GOOGLE, AMAZON, STARBUCKS, the list of shame goes on and on.

Why oh why can these companies not see that avoiding paying tax in the country where you are earning is a disgrace? This sort of behaviour is... er... hang on. Actually... er... Apple, Google, Amazon, Starbucks, give them a break! These international companies stimulate the UK economy and create much needed jobs. And please can I keep mine, Mr Murdoch, sir?

Let's Parlez Franglais!
avec le late Kilometres Kingston

Numéro 94
Le Royal visit de Camilla à Paris

Camilla: Er... bonjour tout le monde...

Premier bloke français dans crowd: Blimey, le Lady Diana n'a pas âgée très well!

Camilla: Non, je suis Camilla, le Duchess de Cornwall.

Première femme française dans crowd: Qui?

Camilla: La femme de Prince Charles.

Deuxième bloke français: Ah, quel dommage! Nous were hoping pour la fruity Kate avec sa bump.

Premier bloke français: Ou la fruity Pippa avec la derrière de nos rêves! Ooh la la!

Première femme française: Taisez-vous up! Vous ne standez pas une chance avec fruity Pippa. Elle est hors de votre league, Monsieur Saddo!

Camilla: Er... Avez-vous come far?

Deuxième femme française: Êtes-vous sure que vous n'êtes pas Helen Mirren? Nous aimons beaucoup le Skyfall.

Deuxième bloke français: Non, non, non, c'était Judi Dench dans le Skyfall avec Monsieur Jacques Bond!

Premier bloke français: Pardonnez-mois, but vous are having un moment senior! La femme avec Monsieur Bond était la Reine de Grande Bretagne – Elizabeth, falling hors du sky avec la parachute dans le stadium Olympique! Êtes-vous la Reine?

Camilla: Er... Anyone got un fag? Je suis gasping pour un gaspeur!

Homme égyptien dans le crowd: Bien sûr! Et puis-je aussi giver vous un lift a la Ritz dans ma chauffeur-driven voiture?

Camilla: Pas fugging likely!

©Let's parlez franglais 2013.

"Darling, of course I didn't realise you were so unhappy"

From The Message Boards

Members of the online community respond to the major issues of the day...

KFC launches boneless chicken

I see that KFC (that's Kentucky Fried Chicken in old money) are introducing drumsticks without the "sticks" because "younger people don't tend to be fans of bones" and have "grown up on nuggets". Speaking as a former younger person the only nugget I ever ate was that chewy pink and white stuff. It pulled your fillings out but I don't recall finding any bones! – **Bogbrush**

It's nougat, not "nugget". – **Jon**

Apologies Jonno! – **Bogbrush**

Pleb. – **Jon**

You may have read about the protester in the chicken suit who was attacked at the Trowbridge KFC recently. You will not, however, have heard about my own protest, thanks to the total media blackout surrounding my activities. On this occasion my beige body tube (which normally represents the wagging finger of the nanny state) was adapted to form a chicken's neck. My friend Cedric (representing unethical industrial farmers) wrung the neck with a series of vigorous pulls while I emitted loud groans (representing the suffering of the chicken). My costume was willfully misconstrued as obscene by the police, who arrested me after the usual "complaints by the public". On this pretext they confiscated my latest pamphlet, which explains the connection between Colonel Sanders, David Cameron, Lord Coe and Mahmood al-Zarooni. – **Edwin**

i dint reelize the name kfc mean's fryed chickin? not bein funny but how are they aloud to fry chicken's? it must be so paneful for them poor bird's ☹ – **Hayley 321**

i dont usuly ete meat usuly i just hav chip's but i did buy a kfc buckit last year it was nice and the buckit make's a nice ornerment – **colin**

If KFC want some good publicity they should give all the leftover bones to the doctors who are force-feeding Ian Brady during his hunger strike. Then, God willing, he will choke to death and rot in hell with Myra Hindley. – **Rot in hell Myra**

My kids (12 and 14) would never dream of eating these processed monstrosities. Instead they make healthy boneless treats such as rissoles and chicken escalopes, using locally sourced ingredients. I recently introduced them to good old-fashioned faggots and they loved them. Am I wrong to feel rather proud? – **Tim the househusband**

u interduce ur kid's 2 faggot's??? wtf??!! – **dwayne**

Any househusband nonce brings them faggots near my girls I swear Ill do time – **Family man**

Who are the top secret political lovebirds whose illicit affair would rock the nation to its foundations if we were allowed to reveal it?

💕 You decide! Is it... 💕

 A: UKIP supremo Nigel Farage and top Tory Nadine Dorries?

 B: Top Tory pundit Simon Heffer and the Daily Mail's Melanie Phillips?

 C: Home Secretary Theresa May and radical preacher Abu Qatada?

 D: Plebgate's Andrew Mitchell MP and Met supremo Bernard Hogan-Howe?

 E: *Strictly Come Dancing*'s Vince Cable and *Strictly Come Dancing*'s Ann Widdecombe?

 F: TV's Charles Moore and the late Lady Thatcher? *(You're fired. Ed.)*

 # *Dave Snooty* AND HIS NEW PALS

DAVE'S BACK FROM HIS HOLS AND LOOKING RED IN THE FACE . . .

HAVE YOU CAUGHT THE SUN DAVE?

NUMBER TEN SEX TORY !!!

NO - BUT I'VE READ THE MAIL ON SUNDAY !!!

I CAN'T BELIEVE IT - A COUPLE OF OUR HIGH-PROFILE CHUMS PLAYING 'HUNT THE SAUSAGE' UNDER OUR NOSES !

DROPPED JAW

AND THE TRULY **INCREDIBLE** THING IS . . .

IT ISN'T BORIS !!!

HALO

ONE COCK-UP YOU CAN'T BLAME ON ME, EH, READERS?

FLIES DONE UP !!!

WITH DAVE IN CHARGE IT'S JUST ONE FLING AFTER ANOTHER, EH, READERS !?!

NEVER TOO OLD

A new love story by Dame Sylvie Krin, author of *Heir of Sorrows* and *Duchess of Hearts*

THE STORY SO FAR: Octogenarian tycoon Rupert Murdoch is under pressure on all fronts as his empire crumbles around him. But surely he will find solace at home? Now read on...

"**D**RINK this, old man, then go to bed." The brittle voice of his young Chinese firecracker wife grated on Rupert's weary nerves, as he meekly sipped the rejuvenating potion of Blowfish Bladder, Tiger Testosterone, Golden Monkey Gonad and Horlicks, all served up in a Ming Campbell Dynasty china bowl.

"But, Wend," he remonstrated, "it's only six o'clock in the evening. I want to stay up for the Fox News Rabid Round-up Show with Brad Barking and Katy Krazy."

"No," she commanded. "Far too exciting. Bad for your heart. And no tweeting whilst I do lesson in advanced Hakjitsu next door." And with a menacing, but playful, shadow kick to his elderly head, Wendi span out of the room, leaving the world's most powerful man alone with his thoughts.

Rupert looked at himself in the ornate 18th-century Louis The Roux mirror and sighed heavily.

What was he doing sitting here in a silver shell-suit with an "I ♥ Justin Bieber" baseball cap on his head? He should be out on the world stage at the centre of the global action, basking in the international limelight... not cooped up here in his penthouse like a dopy dingo in the doghouse down at Goolagong Gulch!

Jeez, was he sick of being told what to do? Lord Bloody Leveson, the nosy coppers, his useless children, the shite-talking shareholders, and now, worst of all, his one-time sweet-lotus-blossom-turned-poisonous-dragon-lady...

And suddenly, in a flash, his mind was made up. The media mogul whose decisiveness was the stuff of legend had come to an epiphanic conclusion. Wasn't he the man who had defied the British establishment when he had launched the Bum newspaper and filled it with topless Sheilas? Yes! Wasn't he the man who had singlehandedly destroyed the British Trade Unions when he had printed the Bumday Times at his new Wappinglies print factory? Yes, again! Wasn't he the man who had crushed the BBC with his Sky Sport Extra Movie Plus One On The Go channel package? Yes, a-bloody-gain!

He was still the same bonzer bruiser from the billabong, the kick-ass cobber from Kangaroo Creek... and from now on **he** was going to set the agenda, call the shots, give the orders...

"You in bed yet, Lupert?" came a high-pitched voice from beyond the Tim Ricepaper screen.

"Just going, my little sour and sour pork ball," he replied softly under his breath, reaching for his Complete Toshiba tablet on which he had secretly been tweeting ever since Wendi had thrown his mobile phone in the piranha tank – where it had been ripped apart by the voracious piscine pets Andy and Rebekah...

Rupert's wrinkled fingers tapped furiously on the highly polished screen: "Wall Street Journal talking good sense on EU/US trade deal. Btw, have fired Wendi Deng as wife."

RUPERT wasn't so sure that announcing the end of his marriage on Twitter was such a good idea now that he was hiding under the table in the offices of top Manhattan divorce lawyers Shyster, Shyster and Kruk, as the shrill screams of his soon-to-be ex-wife filled the air from the other side of the locked door.

"You let me in, Lupert! You in big trouble."

The soothing voice of senior partner Morty Shyster attempted to placate the furious "woman scorned" whose fist was even now punching holes in a shower of splinters through the thick oak door of his suite.

"Really, Ms Deng, I must ask you to restrain yourself and leave the building. The divorce laws of the state of New York stipulate quite clearly that you are not allowed to kick your ex-husband very hard in the groinal area..."

"You owe me big time, unglateful old man! I save your rife from assassin with custard pie!!! I take you to creaners."

The iron bolts on the office door were beginning to strain beneath the repeated hammer blows of the Mandarin mistress of the martial arts. From under the table, the fearless chairman of the biggest news corporation in the galaxy instructed his legal representative.

"Do something, Shyster. Remind her about the pre-nup!"

But Wendi had overheard him. "What plee-nup? I don't lemember anything. Just like you, Lupert, I lemember nothing!" Her ironic cackle of laughter resounded around the panelled walls like the cry of a triumphant banshee across the wild Mongolian plains.

Rupert suddenly felt very old. Very, very old indeed...

(To be continued...)

"It's only my opinion, but I really don't think Sir Ranulph can afford to lose much more to frostbite"

BLAIR DENIES WENDI AFFAIR RUMOUR

It's Rupert I wanted to get into bed with

SUPERMODELS

KERBER

POETRY CORNER

**In Memoriam
Clive Dunn (1920-2012)**

So. Farewell
Then
Clive Dunn,
Corporal Jones in
Dad's Army.

"Don't panic!"
"Permission to speak,
Sir."
"They don't like it
Up 'em."

Yes, those were
Your catchphrases.

It was the
Golden Age of
Comedy.
And we shall
Not see your
Like again.

Except on BBC
Two most Sundays
And on BBC
iPlayer.

E.J. Thribb (17½)

**In Memoriam
Derek Watkins,
trumpeter**

So. Farewell
Then Derek Watkins.

You played trumpet
On every Bond
Soundtrack from
Dr No to Skyfall.

Now you have
Been summoned
By the last
Trumpet of all.

Can you play
The harp?

E.J. Thribb (0017½)

**Lines on the Decision to Phase
out The Liverpool Care
Pathway**

So. Farewell
Then
The Liverpool Care
Pathway.

You are being
killed off.

In a hurry.

Like the
Patients under
Your system.

E.J. Thribb
(17½ Hours to Die)

IT'S THE SUMMER OF LOVE!

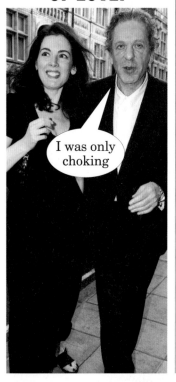

I was only choking

LADIES AND GENTLEMEN. IF YOU'D LIKE TO LOOK OUT OF THE WINDOW, THERE'S A SMALL EXTRA CHARGE RYANAIR

WORLD CUP SPECIAL

BRAZIL SETS IT- SELF ALIGHT WITH FLAIR AND STYLE

by Football Staff **E.I. Adidas**, Our Man Watching It On The Telly In London and Pretending He Is There

ONCE again Brazil has demonstrated that when it comes to riots about football, there is no country to beat them. They are world class protestors with passion and skill in depth.

They are mobile, flexible, agile and speedy, unexpectedly popping up all over the country and creating mayhem.

Already their popular Samba-style of political agitation has shown up the pedestrian quality of rioting nations such as Turkey, who the media has already forgotten in the glow of burning cities like São Paulo.

CLUB FOOTBALLERS

And what about Britain? Why can't we produce world class rioters when we actually invented rioting and gave it to the world? But that is perhaps a question for another day. For now everyone is asking, "Can the Brazilian rioters be beaten?"

The answer from the chief of police yesterday was "Yes. With very Big Batons."

ASSAD 'IT WAS JUST A PLAYFUL TIFF'

by Our Diplomatic Staff **Al Eppo**

THE President of Syria has defended his conduct in the recent civil war saying, "I know the pictures look horrific, but they don't tell the true story.

"I wasn't trying to throttle the opposition, I was merely trying to make my point about the future of the country's children."

He continued, "The reason that there are pictures of women crying is not because I have murdered their relatives, it is because they don't like arguments and were upset by confrontation."

Ass-Adman

He concluded, "We will resolve the conflict by the time I get home".

Ancient bones found in Somerset field

by Our Entire Staff

THOUSANDS of BBC camera crews converged yesterday on a quiet corner of rural Somerset, in order to film the disinterment of a pile of old bones believed to be thousands of years old, possibly dating back to the Stones Age.

"It is definitely one of the most exciting archaeological finds made for decades," said one leading BBC expert, Professor John Humphrys, who is believed to be nearly as old as the bones which the BBC's history team have unearthed.

Old Father Time Team

All BBC programmes were suspended for several hours to allow non-stop coverage of this astonishing breakthrough in palaeo-gerontology.

Said Humphrys, "The skulls of these skeletal figures are truly extraordinary, if a little scary.

But, considering their incredible age, it is amazing how much of them remains reasonably intact.

"Indeed, I had the immense privilege of being allowed an exclusive interview with what the archaeologists have dubbed *homo jaggerensis*.

"Unfortunately, the pile of bones was too old to remember anything of what everyday life was like in the Stones Age because it was all, frankly, you know, I mean, too long ago, man."

Professor John Humphrys is 3,412.

MARRIAGE ISN'T WORKING

I'M BETTER OFF ON MY OWN

"It's not the subtlest way for Saatchi to announce his divorce"

OBAMA LAYS IT ON THE LINE OVER SYRIA

Assad's a ruthless tyrant who rules by fear and poisons his own people

Yes, but he must have some bad points too

'ICH BIN EIN DUBLINER'
U.S. President's historic boast

by Our Irish Staff **Belfast Mooney**

ON THE eve of the global G8 summit, President Obama last night made a surprise stop-off in Belfast to reveal to an astonished world that he had just discovered that he is descended from Irish ancestors.

"I am proud to tell you," he told a crowd of cheering schoolchildren, "that I am one of the O'Bamas of Ballyuseful.

"My great-great-grandfather, old Hussein O'Bama, was well-known for his brewing of Irish potato vodka in the early part of the 19th century and his prowess in the line-dance.

"And my great-aunt Yasmin Alibhai-O'Bama was the muse to W.B. Yeats and the inspiration for his great poem *The Drones of Killymanjaro*.

"I am overjoyed to become the 94th American President who has discovered his Irish roots, and I am thus qualified to talk what I believe we Irishmen know as 'the blarney' with the best of them."

The President concluded, "And a slamdunk top of the evenin' to you all".

Late News

G185 MEETING 'A ROARING SUCCESS'

A meeting of all the world's nations outside the G8 has been deemed a triumph after it came up with a series of consensual accords.

The G185 – which account for 50% of the world's GDP – agreed that the top eight industrial nations generally ignore the rest of the world and are only interested in "feathering their own nest".

NEW DRESS-DOWN G8 SUMMIT

That New Girl Guide Oath in Full

OLD OATH

"I promise that I will do my best to love my God, to serve the Queen and my country, to help other people and to keep the Guide law."

NEW OATH

"You know, in a very real sense, that I will set as my target a genuine aspiration to deliver a programme of personal growth including my belief systems, and to roll out a full range of commitments to participating in the activities of my local community, with special reference to those who may be in particular need of assistance, subject of course to the assessments of fully-qualified health and safety advisers acting in co-operation with the Guide movement, and to follow all the Guidelines laid down by the movement as these are subject to annual revision. Oh yes, and I promise not to be rude about the Queen because frankly she is an old woman and she used to be a Girl Guide herself back in the bad old days when the Guides were a nationalistic, chauvinistic, ideological, quasi-fascist movement like the Hitler Youth."

Dear Occupier

POETRY CORNER

Lines on the 70th anniversary of the Dambusters raid

So. It is
Seventy years
Since 617 squadron
Carried out its
Daring raid on the
Ruhr Valley
Dams.

Let us remember
Those brave
Men. But
Forget the name
Of Guy Gibson's
Dog.

All together now,
Da-da-da
Da-da
Di-da-di-da
Etc...

E.J. Thribb (17½ repeats on the History Channel)

DAMBUSTER ANNIVERSARY FLYPAST

For you, Tommy, ze war is never over!

75

EXCLUSIVE TO ALL PAPERS

UNIVERSAL CONDEMNATION OF JOHN INVERDALE

by Our Men's Double Standards Staff

John: Looker

THERE has rightly been widespread condemnation today of John Inverdale's highly sexist comments about the Wimbledon women's final winner Marion Bartoli's looks.

It is simply astonishing to this newspaper that anyone in the media could objectify and judge female tennis players according to their looks.

When during Wimbledon fortnight we run fruity photos of Maria Sharapova stretching for a ball so she's showing some frilly knickers we do so to celebrate her sporting prowess and not to give our readers a cheap thrill because she's hotter than a supermodel showering naked whilst eating a Cornetto.

Equally, when we've not run any photos of Marion Bartoli ever that isn't because we don't think she is attractive, no, we have chosen not to run those photos to show how we value and appreciate her sporting prowess.

That's why we insist John Inverdale immediately stop making vile outdated sexist remarks about the deliciously fruity ladies of Wimbledon fortnight.

Phwoar! Sharapova, eh! I would! Bartoli? No way!

ON OTHER PAGES

● Photos of fruity tennis players at Wimbledon
● No photos of Marion Bartoli

We've waited 77 years and finally...

...it's a sunny weekend

Daily Mail, Monday July 8, 2013

THE WORLD'S WORST COLUMNIST

Why oh why I now love Andy Murray

By Max Hastings

I'VE NEVER liked Andy Murray very much and I've never really liked tennis either. Still, there are times when one has to cast aside one's prejudices and think again.

Sunday 7th July was just such a moment, when the phone rang and Paul Dacre asked me to write a 1,000-word piece on Andy Murray for the Daily Mail.

Could I do it? Could I triumph against all the odds and overcome some very strong competition to produce the single worst piece about Wimbledon 2013.

Yes! In the end, it was a close-run thing and it was torture to read, but the entire British public woke up on Monday morning to discover that it wasn't a dream – the long wait was over and at long last a British journalist had given them a piece that was truly world class in its *(cont. p. 94)*

Tomorrow: *Why oh why is it so hot? by Max "Temperature" Hastings.*

"This is hopeless... my internet is not working"

What is sunshine?

For those of the population of Britain who have never experienced this strange phenomenon before:

Sunshine is direct sunlight (electromagnetic radiation) from 'the Sun' – usually in a cloudless blue sky – especially when over a comparatively large area.

Apology

IN RECENT weeks, in common with all other newspapers and media in general, we may have given the impression that we like the summer to be sunny, dry and hot and not cold, wet and miserable. Headlines such as 'WHERE'S OUR BARBECUE SUMMER?' and 'IT'S BRITISH BUMMERTIME AGAIN' may have led some readers to believe that we were in some way fed up with the prevailing temperate climate. We now realise that the above sentiment is absolute nonsense, and that the recent hot weather has in fact been not merely undesirable but frankly unbearable. We hope that headlines such as 'PHEW, WHAT A KILLER' and 'LONG MAY IT RAIN' will rectify any confusion caused by our previous coverage of the weather.

John Inverdale's Guide to History's Greatest Women

BOADICEA
Definitely overcompensating for her thick arms. Norfolk lass, of course, but we can't all be from Malibu or suchlike.

QUEEN VICTORIA
Dumpy girl. Probably fretted about that, which is why she took over India.

EMILY WILDING DAVISON
Very sad, ending up under that horse like that. Hadn't been asked out to a dance, is my diagnosis.

ROSA PARKS
Stayed sitting on the bus – wanted not to show her backside to anyone, I reckon. Nevertheless, a great achievement and a turning point in history.

FLORENCE NIGHTINGALE
Tremendous administrator, magnificent nurse, absolutely enormous eyebrows. Really bushy, they were. She got into medicine trying to find a cure, if memory serves.

MARIE CURIE
Very striking profile, Curie. Nose like a kukri knife. Still, it gave her the courage to stay in the lab and win the Nobel.

JANE AUSTEN
Revolutionised the British novel, but a complete stranger to the word 'moisturiser'. If she gets on the tenner, there'll be a lot of folks asking for their change in fivers, I'll bet!

(That's enough. Ed!)

Politicians Accuse Each Other of Playing Party Politics

by Our Political Staff **Polly Tix**

THERE were extraordinary scenes in the House of Commons yesterday during a debate about the failures of the National Health Service.

Politicians from all sides accused each other of ignoring the issue and "playing party politics".

Said one Conservative MP, "Accusing me of playing party politics is clearly just playing party politics, and I really want to focus on the Health Service and what the other party has done to ruin it."

A Labour MP hit back saying, "How dare he deny playing party politics? This is a typical Tory tactic to divert attention from the important issue, which is the Health Service, and what the other party has done to ruin it."

A Lib Dem MP, however, interjected, "This is typical of the two main parties playing party politics, instead of focusing on the important issue, which is the Health Service and what they've both done to ruin it."

"I'm afraid there's a lot of it about, Mr Smith. Polish is an extremely difficult language"

U.S. SPYING ON EUROPE

I always said I would listen to the American people…

…just didn't mention I'd be listening to the French, German and British too

PICK YOUR OWN REASON FOR NOT PICKING FRUIT

a) BETTER OFF CLAIMING BENEFITS
b) CAN'T BE BOTHERED
c) WHAT'S FRUIT?

K.J.Lamb

OBAMA VISITS MANDELA CELL ON ROBBEN ISLAND

This'll be perfect for Snowden

SNOWDEN APPLIES FOR ASYLUM

by Our Man in Moscow Airport **Ivan O'Idea**

NSA whistleblower Edward Snowden has confirmed that he has withdrawn his request for asylum in Russia and decided instead to apply for asylum in America.

"Only America can protect me from a country where everyone is spied on by the State and dissidents are locked away without trial," said the *(cont. p. 94)*

what's bugging you? *GCHQ*

George Leigh

Those Iranian presidential election results in full

The winner with 105 percent of the vote was the extreme moderate hard-line fundamentalist reform candidate Dr Rowhardlini, whose popular platform of being not quite as extreme as any of the other candidates secured him a landslide victory.

His nearest rival, the even more hardline, not at all moderate, extremist fundamentalist, Imam Masmurdah, failed to attract much support, with his manifesto promising to hang half the population from cranes as a deterrent to the other half.

Dr Rowhardlini has promised a new dawn for Iran, with an array of progressive, liberal reformist policies, such as developing nuclear weapons, destroying Israel, defying the great Satan in its attempts to undermine Islamicist theocracy, and generally giving the outside world an impression of being thoroughly moderate, sensible, pragmatic and not at all bonkers.

Dr Rowhardlini was congratulated on his victory by his predecessor as President, Dr Ahmedinajacket, who said, "Of course, it doesn't really matter who wins these elections because the country is still run by the Supreme Leader, the Ayatollah Khomeini Jong Il. *(Is this right? Ed.)*

DID PRINCE PHILIP TRY TO KILL THE DUKE OF EDINBURGH?

By Our Conspiracy Staff **Mohammed Al-Fayed**

OF COURSE he fuggin' did. It was all a conspiracy. Prince Philip was in on it with MI5, CIA, Mossad and Dignitas.

Yes, Prince Philip had his fuggin' sights set on the Duke Of Edinburgh from the start, got him to walk around in the fuggin' freezing fuggy weather, standing like a silly fugger watching the Red Arrows fuggin' about.

Someone had better arrest the fugger now, before Prince Philip finishes the fugger off and *(cont. p. 94)*

Mail Online

Beautiful young medical student with eating disorder dies after taking banned slimming pills. Are today's young women too pressured to be skinny?

PLUS!

▶ Celebrity you've never heard of pours herself into a tiny bikini to flaunt her taut, gym-toned frame on the beach.

▶ Celebrity mum shows off her stunning Size 0 bikini just eight minutes after giving birth.

▶ Celebrity is 'fat and flabby' pics.

▶ 50-year-old actress SLAMMED for being a 50-year-old woman.

ME AND MY SPOON

THIS WEEK

CARA DELEVINGNE

Do spoons feature prominently in your life?
Ha ha ha ha.

Do you have a favourite type of spoon, say, one that can be used for recreational purposes?
Ha ha ha ha.

Do you use spoons regularly? Or just socially?
Ha ha ha ha.

As a role model for young women, do you feel your spoon habit sends out the right message?
Ha ha ha ha.

Has anything amusing ever happened to you involving a spoon and some sachets of mystery white powder?
You'll have to ask my solicitor.

WEAPONS This way up *ENJOY RESPONSIBLY*

Bernie

FALKIRK ROW INTENSIFIES

UNITE have defended themselves against allegations of packing local Labour parties with non-existent members.

"Fictional people have a right to be heard too," said local organiser Gerry Mander. "The fact they don't exist doesn't mean that they don't care for the rights of ordinary working people."

"Non-existent people are more likely to be Labour members, as they are often less well-off than real people," said secretary Phil Ballots. "Most of them are dead, and many of them have stupid names, which ensures that they live on the fringes of society. The important thing is that they support genuine Labour candidates like my girlfriend Jilly Shooin."

Those Members in Full

I.M. Notreal, Vic Titious, Dee Ceased, U. Nite
(That's enough names. Ed.)

"The traditional cosy Sunday night escapism: The naked body of a young girl… A child goes missing… A prostitute is murdered… A serial killer terrorises a…"

THAT TOM WATSON RESIGNATION LETTER IN FULL

Dear Ed Miliband,

I said that I'd stay with you as general election coordinator within the Shadow Cabinet as long as I thought you would be useful to me. Now that it is clear you are no longer useful to me or anyone else, the time has come for me to stand down.

As you know, I offered my resignation on Tuesday and you are so pathetically weak that you asked me to reconsider. It is that uniquely pathetic weakness which you possess which I have always admired.

Yet it's not the unattributed shadow cabinet briefings from your bastard mates around Falkirk that have convinced me to go. I believe the Falkirk report should be published – in full – and the whole truth told. I've still not seen the report and I would not want to prejudge in any way something I know with 100% certainty will, from start to finish, be a tissue of Blairite lies designed to smear Len McClusky and myself.

Having resigned a couple of times before, I know how puckish lobby hacks might choose to misconstrue my departure. So, to make it harder for them, let me say this: I'm proud of your Buddha-like qualities of ineptitude as you blunder from crisis to crisis like the blindfolded drunk driver steering a runaway clown car through a minefield. You're my friend and leader, and I'm going to do all I can to destroy you by 2015.

John Humphrys asked me why you were not at Glastonbury with me this weekend. He does have a point, it's so much easier to imagine you as Prime Minister when on hallucinogenic drugs. If you'd been with me, there's no way you'd be handing over the Falkirk report to the police… I mean, how square can you get daddy-o; The Police!? They haven't had a hit in years. Haven't you heard of the Arctic Monkeys, The XX, Haim or Drenge?

Yours sincerely, TOM WATSON

Channel 4 deny 'ratings chasing'

by Our Media Staff
Des Perate

A spokeschild for Channel 4 today denied that their latest hit show *The Man With the 10-stone Testicles* was in any way a shameless attempt to boost otherwise flagging ratings with a bottom-of-the-barrel medical infotainment programme.

"This was a public service broadcast for all those men who have 10-stone testicles, er, one," said the spokeschild, adding, "Blimey, have you seen them? They're enormous, they're like space-hoppers, only bigger, and you can still see them now on 4oD!"

The spokeschild went on to say, "People say all our shows are embarrassing bollocks, but in fact that's only one show."

He explained that if Channel 4 was just chasing ratings with "freak show-style" programming, they wouldn't have made next week's moving and highbrow documentary *The Dwarf Siamese Twin Bearded Ladies* and the forthcoming BAFTA-tipped reality strand, *My Big Fat Gypsy Haemorrhoid*.

A Channel 4 insider said, "Everyone's afraid to mention the Elephant Man in the room, but we've got no programme ideas whatsoever."

Channel 4 Announce 'Call To Prayer For Viewers'

by Our Media Staff
Ian Creasingly-Desperate

A spokestoddler for Channel 4 announced the exciting new summer line-up. He said, "We're not just trying to shock people by broadcasting a call to prayer from a mosque. This is a properly thought-out and considered response to today's multi-cultural, multi-faith and, let's be honest, multi-channel society, where people are free to watch whatever they like and turn off Channel 4."

Those Ramadan programmes in full

● *Come Don't Dine With Me*
● *Countdown Till Sunset*
● *Meal Or No Meal*

The Adventures of Mr Milibean

Fountain & Jamieson

How that BBC £369 million pay-off system worked in full

STAGE ONE

McKinsey win £5 million contract to find suitable candidate for new BBC post of Head of Digital Platform Resource Planning (Regional).

STAGE TWO

After nine-month recruitment process costing £7.5 million, the successful applicant (Phil Pocket, pictured above) is identified and negotiates a £12.3 million package, including salary, bonus, pension and free tickets to Glastonbury.

STAGE THREE

The new head of DPRP(R) takes up his post in TV Centre White City, but is immediately moved to BBC Salford, necessitating a full rehousing and redeployment package costing £16.3 million.

STAGE FOUR

After serving six months in his post and having recruited a 25-person strong support staff, it becomes clear that the new head of DPRP(R) is, in the words of a confidential £19 million assessment by Accenture, "absolutely bloody useless". Their consultancy report concludes "our investigation also shows that there is no possible functional need for this post or indeed this whole department".

STAGE FIVE

Acting on the Accenture report, a senior BBC management committee decides that the DPRP(R) should be renamed and given a new remit. This new Regional Resource Platform Planning (Digital) or RRPP(D) is charged with taking on 47 more staff at a cost of £26 million to map out ways of extending the old department's responsibilities.

STAGE SIX

When the management committee suggested that Capita be hired to find a new head for the newly-reconstructed department, the existing head, Pocket, calls in his lawyers who threaten to take the BBC before an industrial tribunal, demanding compensation of £37 million for his loss of office, hurt feelings and enforced move back to London (plus of course loss of free tickets to Glastonbury).

STAGE SEVEN

In face of this threat, the old head of DPRP(R) is appointed to succeed himself as head of the new RRPP(D), at an increased salary of £354,000 a year, plus augmented bonus and pension entitlements, plus tickets for Glastonbury. This is to cover the wide range of additional responsibilities entailed in running the new department.

STAGE EIGHT

After another six months, it is clear that the new head of RRPP(D) is even more useless in this new post than he was in the old one. His decision to purchase a £100 million Digitised Archival Audio-Visual Resource Data Management System is found by the National Audit Office to have been a "total waste of licence-payers' money" because no one had any idea what it was intended to do or why.

STAGE NINE

At a top-level secret meeting between the Chairman of the BBC Trust Lord Patten and the Director-General Lord Hall, it is decided that "we've got to sack this totally incompetent idiot whatever it costs".

By the time a team of accountants, brought in from PwC at a cost of £42 million, has worked out the full redundancy package for Pocket and his entire department, the final bill works out at £369 million.

UPDATE

Phil Pocket, the former head of the BBC's prestigious Regional Resource Planning Platform (Digital), is to be paid $8 million a year in his new job as Editor-in-Chief of one of the US's most influential newspapers, the New Dworkin Bee and Advertiser.

NEW CIGARETTE PACKAGING UNVEILED

CIGARETTE manufacturers have accepted a compromise agreement which would see them featuring horrific images of David Cameron with Lynton Crosby on cigarette packets.

"These are very graphic and frightening images which should bring home to kids the effects of smoking, as they'll lead to gasping, shortness of breath, blurred vision and the need to cough your guts up." *(Rotters)*

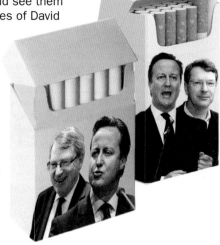

Cigarette companies find 'no link'

Cigarette companies say despite extensive studies they can find no causal link between David Cameron, and Lynton Crosby.

"For some time anti-smoking groups have claimed the fact David Cameron is a 'passive pollster' means he inhales noxious gasses emitted by his advisers on a daily basis," said an ashen-faced fag maker, yesterday.

"However, we can find no evidence that David Cameron's sweating, shortness of breath and shaking hands have anything to do with him taking in the thoughts of an angry Australian telling him to cut the happy clappy bullshit, you posh drongo, and start crushing more poor people.

"The health police'll be saying there's a link between cigarette smoking and lung cancer next."

A Doctor Doesn't Write

AS A doctor, I'm often asked, "Will you shut up about what's going wrong in this hospital in return for a large sum of money?"

The simple answer is "Yes".

© A Doctor 2013

WHAT'S GOING ON IN EGYPT?

We don't know.

ON OTHER PAGES ● Our correspondents ask a lot of other people who don't know what's going on ● Our photographers take confused photos of people milling around being angry ● British government takes steps to avoid Egypt-style coup by sacking all remaining soldiers.

EGYPT – THEN AND NOW

2012

Hooray – Morsi elected

2013

Hooray – Morsi ousted

Tony Blair
Writes For The Eye

MANY in the press have questioned the legitimacy of the Egyptian Army deposing the popularly elected Muslim Brotherhood government of President Morsi. They question whether such a coup can ever be justified.

But I say to them what gives the Egyptian army's actions legitimacy is the fact that over a million ordinary people took to the streets of Cairo to protest about a government so blinded by ideology it had lost the popular mandate… just as in February of 2003 over a million people took to the streets of London to protest against a government which also had become so blinded by ideology it had lost its popular mandate…

Um…

And that's why I'm, er… all for popular rule by the mob… except when… er… can I have my cheque please?

Thank you.

RIDDLE OF THE SPHINX

What's good unless it's bad?

Democracy

Historic script found

A never before seen script for an episode of 'Yes, Prime Minister' from the 1980s has been found, and the Eye is delighted to share an excerpt with readers

Sir Humphrey: Prime Minister, you appear to be recommending the disc jockey, Mr James Savile for a knighthood.

Bernard: …for the fifth time.

Prime Minister: Yes, Humphrey, but only because you've said 'no' four times.

(Audience laughter)

Bernard: But there is a reason for that Prime Minister...

Sir Humphrey: We feel that, as a candidate for such an honour, there are questions surrounding Mr Savile's suitability, due to his inappropriate behaviour when in the vicinity, of, well, how can I put this, those persons younger and more attractive than himself.

Bernard: Isn't that everybody?

(More audience laughter)

Prime Minister: But he does a huge amount for charity... And he spends Christmas with me at Chequers.

Sir Humphrey *(wryly)***:** I suppose that counts as charity.

(Even more audience laughter)

Sir Humphrey: But not withstanding his philanthropic propensities, and all-round beneficence vis à vis the paraplegic and other communities, there is surely a potential risk that he may have overstepped the boundaries between the acceptable and the unacceptable...

(Audience begin laughing and prepare to applaud trademark long sentence by Sir Humphrey)

Sir Humphrey *(cont.)***:** ...in the area of interpersonal relationships with the recipients of his charitable impulses...

Prime Minister: I don't understand.

Bernard: We think he might be a paedo.

(Ecstatic audience laughter)

Sir Humphrey: Thank you, Bernard.

Prime Minister: I have no idea what you're talking about, nor do I want to know. He's hugely popular and I would like to be too. Give him the knighthood.

Sir Humphrey: Yes, Prime Minister.

(Audience die laughing)

CROWDED DELIVERY ROOM WELCOMES ROYAL BABY

K.J.Lamb

What You Missed

TV (All channels)

Phil Airtime: Thanks, well the situation here is that we're all still waiting for news and joining me now is MaryLou Blondberg, the royal correspondent for Oregon's prestigious NBGTV channel. MaryLou, what's your view of what's going on?

Blondberg: I have with me here Phil Airtime, the royal correspondent for the prestigious British Sky ITV Broadcasting Corporation. Phil, what's your feeling about the events as they are unfolding?

Airtime: There's a lot of speculation going on, MaryLou, but could you speculate for me as to how long the speculation is going to go on?

MaryLou: It's too early to give any precise details about the speculation, but what I can do is ask you, Phil, how *you* feel about all this speculation?

Airtime: Good question, MaryLou. And I'd like to ask you if you think there is too much speculation?

MaryLou: I have to interrupt you there, Phil, as we're being told that a spokesman is coming out of the hospital to tell us that there is no news at all…

Airtime: Can I interrupt you there, MaryLou, to tell viewers that we're all still waiting for news and joining me now is MaryLou Blondberg from Oregon's *(cont. for 94 hours).*

The Eye's Controversial New Columnist

The columnist who pushes his dog on wheels to the limit

This week I am very angry at being asked to write about the so-called royal birth. I have no idea why I of all people should be asked to write about such a piece of irrelevant frippery. Has the world gone baby mad? I have made my protest in the strongest terms, and I'm glad this paper's proprietor is just as angry as me. If I can quote from his general e-mail to the staff: "It seems the only thing that is significant about this 'personage' is the fact it is a baby! Cute and cuddly it may be, but it hasn't demonstrated any talent or abilities yet, and it will soon learn that if it doesn't grow up and toe the line pronto, then it will be deposed forthwith."

ADDENDUM: Upon re-reading the angry e-mail, I have realised that it's not concerning the royal baby at all. So basically what my column is trying to say is: *Three cheers for Kate Middleton! (cont. page 94)*

POETRY CORNER

Lines on the Failure of the Poet Laureate to Write a Poem Celebrating the Birth of the Royal Baby

So. Carol Ann Duffy.

The muse has Deserted you.

Er... Um...
Er...
Me too.

> E.J. Thribby (17½ years of writer's block)

"Who's going to cut the cord?"

-PILBROW-

The Daily Jelly Torygraph

Friday, 9 August 2013

JELLYFISH MENACE THREATENS HOLIDAYMAKERS

By Our Marine Staff Marina Warner and Angelina Joliefish

HUGE numbers of pictures of fruity girls in bikinis were today spotted in all newspapers, as editors strove to cope with the invasion of killer jellyfish which are now threatening Britain's beaches.

Said one leading editor, "Frankly, we welcome the arrival of these maritime monsters, since they provide us with an excellent excuse to print huge pictures of fruity girls in skimpy beachwear of the type who might or might not be threatened by these deadly denizens of the deep."

Said another editor, "We don't even have to wait until the end of August now to put in pictures of fruity girls celebrating their A-Level results – although we will, of course, be doing that as well."

Daily Mail, Friday July 26, 2013

THE WORLD'S WORST COLUMNIST

Why oh why aren't there any wasps?

Asks Max Hastings

THE sun is shining. The sky is blue. Your picnic is laid out on the travel blanket on the grass. And yet something is missing.

Where, you ask, is the familiar, comforting whine of the British wasp buzzing around your head and alighting on your sandwich?

What has gone wrong to ruin the pleasure of the traditional British summer?

Who has killed off our flying friends to the detriment of every wasp lover in the nation?

The finger points squarely at the hated European Union and Brussels, whose anti-wasp directives have, as ever, spoilt the pleasures of *(This is brilliant. Have some more money. Ed.)*

© *Mad Max Hastings, 2013.*

EXCLUSIVE TO ALL PAPERS

A-LEVEL RESULTS SPELL DISAPPOINTMENT FOR MANY

by Our Education Staff **Ed Ucation**

This year's A-Levels have seen many not achieve the hoped-for results.

Said one editor, "We were expecting to put pictures of fruity girls hugging on the front page. Instead, tougher marking has meant there are fewer fruity girls squealing with delight."

He added, "The fruity girls with poorer results may not have got

onto their front page of choice, but may well get into page 3 through clearing."

LATEST BABY LATEST

IT'S THE XXXX FACTOR!

By our Baby Correspondent, M. Brionic

THE WORLD's media gathered anxiously around Simon Cowell's luxury yacht last night as they awaited news of the most famous baby since last week.

Cowell was believed to be on the yacht, hiding from the press and more importantly from his friend Andrew Silverman, whose wife is now ten weeks pregnant. When asked if the baby was his, he said, "It's a No... Comment from me, but a yes from everyone else." This means that Lauren Silverman, 36, goes through to the next round where she'll sign a contract with Cowell's management group, after which she will never be heard of again.

David Cameron tweeted, "This is wonderful news, you've cheered up the whole nation." Ed Miliband added, "Has something happened – should I be tweeting about it?"

With only seven months to go until the birth, there is a betting frenzy underway to guess the name of the lovechild.

INSIDE: Cowell ready to breastfeed already p9

THOSE ODDS IN FULL

BOY		GIRL
Walliam	2-1	Danniiii
Wall.i.Am	7-1	Dan.i.Am
Ant	EVENS	Amanda
Dec	EVENS	Susan Boyle
Ant'n'Dec	2 in 1	Sinitta
Conceived on Deck	1 on 1	Sharon
Andrew Silverman	100-1	Andrea Silverman

A message from the Mayor of London **Boris Johnson**

Cripes! Have you seen all the hoo-ha over this Weiner chappie who wants to be Mayor of New York? Turns out the fellow has got sex on the brain and has been sending pictures of his John Thomas to various lady friends in the Big Apple!

Good for him! What's all the fuss about? If a mayor can't take the odd private snap of his todger and sext it to a few chums of the female persuasion, what is the world coming to?

Who wants their politicians to be grey, boring and with their trousers on? Not us, surely! I say, vote for Boris and his wonderful wiener (and it isn't weenie!)

Cheerio!
Boris

© The Mayor of London 2013.

"For goodness' sake – now what's their problem?"

DIARY

DR DAVID STARKEY'S A-Z OF EVERYTHING THAT'S WRONG WITH THIS COUNTRY OF OURS

ADELE: For all her hollering and screeching, that overly plump young female doesn't know the foggiest thing about the Tudors. Or the Stuarts, for that matter. Yet they continue to pile her with Oscars and Emmys. And that tells you all you need to know about the pampered liberal elite and its futile attempts to put a sheen on things as this country goes, quite literally, down the drain. I'm very sorry, but that's the way it is.

BEAR, RUPERT: There's nothing you can teach me about Rupert Bear, thank you very much indeed. He's a deeply unpleasant, boring, feeble little creature, addicted to speaking in the most fatuous, simpering doggerel and scrounging without a by-your-leave off the state. So let's not pussyfoot on this issue. That grotesque bear knowingly led a generation of children to think they could get away with doing nothing but prance about while the rest of us slogged out our guts to put afternoon tea on his ill-made woodland table. Well, not any more we won't. My message to Rupert Bear and his so-called pals from Nutwood is clear: put up or shut up. It's as simple as that!

CAMBRIDGE, DUCHESS OF: It would not be going too far to call that ambitious young lady a great fat trollop and whore. At least we can all agree on that. But let me make one further point, if I may, and I want to spell it out in words of one syllable. Kate's even less attractive sister "Pippa" – and what sort of name is THAT, may one ask? – has one of the biggest arses ever seen to waddle its way down the aisle of Westminster Abbey. In fact, I am reliably informed that the Palace minions were up all night before the wedding pushing those ancient pews a yard or two nearer to the walls in order to accommodate her show-off procession up the aisle.

DOCTORS: It pains me to say that it is all part and parcel of our insipid, sentimental, weak and, yes, irredeemably feminised culture that we are now expected to bow down and kow-tow to those men (and, inevitably, women!) who ponce about in white coats and simperingly promise to – and here I quote – "make us better".

Well, you're not going to make me better, chummy. The last time I went to a doctor, I told him to quit whining, stop being a drain on the taxpayer and get a proper job. Let's make no bones about it. When I require a major operation, a doctor is the last person I would run to. Any halfway-decent plumber or handyman could do the same job for a quarter of the price. It's time to face up to the uncomfortable truth that most doctors couldn't even cure a herring. So why do our fatuous politicians of all parties suck up to them, pouring money into every available orifice? It's all "ooh, doctor this" and "ooh, doctor that". Well, I'm very sorry but it's time to face facts.

EMU: It goes without saying that Rod Hull was an immensely respected and highly erudite man of international standing. Yet for many decades it was his great misfortune to be followed everywhere – stalked would not be too strong a word – by an emu. This emu – female, for just this once let's be honest about it – made it her purpose to stick her beak into all his arrangements, messing up every learned discussion upon which he attempted to embark, forcing him to divert his sharp intelligence away from more important matters into some footling piece of damage limitation.

It is symptomatic of our times that Rod Hull and Emu must now always be mentioned in the same breath, as though it is somehow only right that they be remembered on equal terms. Has there ever been a more devastating indictment of the mire of utter unreality into which our increasingly fifth rate nation has sunk?

FLOWERS: Everyone says "Ooh, we love flowers, flowers are so colourful and they smell so nice too". Well, I'm sorry to disappoint you, but NO THEY DO NOT. Not only do they smell rancid, but their colours are revolting and vulgar. But no one has the courage to point it out. For the past hundred-odd years there has been this easy squidgey, liberal consensus in this country that flowers are somehow "pretty". In case you haven't noticed, as a country we have allowed them to run riot over our cities and our countryside. There's no escaping them. They even fug up Regent's Park in central London with their disgusting stench. And why? Because successive governments have been so utterly spineless that no one has had the guts to go round tramping them down and pulling them out. We're in one of the worst financial crises this country has ever faced, for pity's sake – yet you continue to sniff the cyclamen. Frankly, you must be out of your tiny little minds! *(continues on page 94)*

As told to C R A I G   B R O W N

Alice in Wongaland

K.J.Lamb

HS2 BREAKS RECORD

HISTORY was made yesterday, when the budget for the HS2 line accelerated faster than any other comparable high-speed network.

"We knew it was going to lose money at incredible speed," said a spokesman, "but we had no idea it was going to break all records."

The spokesman also discounted allegations there was no actual need for a high-speed network, saying that demand for rail travel had risen sharply in recent weeks.

"There is a huge rise in the number of NIMBYs travelling up and down the country to protest about the countryside being ruined," he explained.

Nursery Times

.... Friday, Once-upon-a-time ....

PRINCE DENIES 'HOMEOPATHY IS WITCHCRAFT'

By Our Royal Staff, **Nicholas Witch**

HIS Royal Highness Prince Charmless has been secretly lobbying the Nurseryland government to try and change their attitudes to the controversial "alternative medicine" which is being widely practised.

Prince Charmless has praised the bona fide medical practitioners who seek to cure ailments by traditional means using remedies such as eye of newt, tongue of dog, adder's fork, blindworm's sting, lizard's leg, root of hemlock and gall of goat.

According to the prince, if used in minute quantities, these substances can have an amazing effect on a wide range of conditions and should be considered alongside more conventional medicine.

When asked for a quote the prince said, "I've been using these cures for years and they haven't done me any harm."

He then added, "Rivet, rivet" before jumping off his lily pad into the pond.

On other pages

● Rumplestiltskin: "I just can't guess the name of the royal baby" **3** ● Mirror, mirror on wall slammed for sexism – "You can't tell people who's the fairest of all," says Contrary Maria **4** ● Gingerbread man fails dope test – traces of banned nutmeg found in fast-as-you-can runner **94**

SUMMER HIGHLIGHTS

TV

The Great British Baked Toff

BBC2

85

The Alternative Rocky Horror Service Book

No. 94 A Service For The Offering Of Credit To The Poor At Affordable Rates Of Interest

The Manager (*Archbishop Welby, for it is he*): We are gathered here today to bless the opening of our new church-based credit facility to assist all those of our brothers and sisters who are unable to keep up with their payments for whatsoever reason that may be.

All: Indeedy doody, for we are all in deep doodah!

THE OFFERING

All: Oh Lord, open thou our credit lines.

Welby: But deliver us from Wonga.

All: Amen.

(The offertory hymn shall then be sung, Hymn 94, "Guide me, o thou great redeemer of the loan")

READING

Reader: Our reading is taken from the Gospel according to St Mark Carney: "And it came to pass that Jesus went up into the temple where he found many money lenders. And he waxed wroth. For he observed that they were charging rates of interest far beyond that which any poor man could pay, even an hundredfold or an thousandfold. And Jesus said unto them, 'I am not going to throw you out of the temple, as you deserve. I am going to set up in competition with you, offering to lend money to the poor at affordable terms, which will cast you out of the temple, using the forces of the free market.' And all the people were sore amazed, and said amongst themselves, 'Who is this man who cometh up with such a brilliant wheeze? Surely he can only be a wizard? But is he serving God or Mammon?' And they went away wagging their heads, and in no certain mind as to what he was up to."

All: This is the word of the Lord King.

Welby: At this point, I must ask the congregation whether they know any just cause or impediment why this scheme should not be permitted to proceed...

Lone voice, Mr M. Giggler: Because the Church of England's £5.5 billion investment fund includes a shareholding in the firm Wonga. And in my view, two Wongas don't make it right!

Welby: I am indebted to you, Mr Giggler. Objection overruled. And now cometh the moment when you must all dig deep into your pockets to raise the necessary capital to get my scheme off the ground – remembering the wise words of Scripture, that it is more blessed to give than receive.

THE PRAYER

Welby: Let us pay.

(The congregation shall then shuffle out of the church, confessing that just now they are "a bit short" and have a lot of "unexpected expenses", but that otherwise it is "a great idea" and they would love to help, but perhaps at another time)

NEW OLD SAYINGS

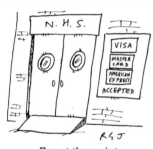

Fee at the point of delivery

TRAFALGAR SQUARE 4TH PLINTH LATEST

Oh look, there's a big blue cock!

Right not to die campaign

By our Health Correspondent
Phil Graves

CAMPAIGNERS who believe in their right not to die when they go into hospital last night received another set back, when even more hospitals were found to be below very basic standards. Said one protestor, "It's about basic human dignity. We should be allowed to choose when we die – not just as soon as we enter a hospital."

A government spokesman however replied, "This is the thin end of the wedge, we can't allow this, otherwise people are going to be talked into not dying by their relatives, and we simply can't afford it."

Health Minister Jeremy Hunt was not available for comment, as he was too busy performing secret, under-cover open heart surgery for the benefit of photographers.

TV Highlights

Call the Mid Staffs

Heart-stopping Sunday night drama in which patients are cheerfully neglected and medical staff work round the clock to make sure they're ignored. Set way back in time – last year, it's great on period detail, which shows the NHS working like it did in the 1950s only with fewer doctors. Based on the famous cooked books by Andy Burnham.

DAILY MAIL, Friday, August 9, 2013

Major investigation uncovers shock secret

by **Ms Ogeny**

A major Daily Mail investigation has blown the lid off sensational claims that women do not age and always look as glamorous as they did in their 20s.

Using these two pictures of Britt Ekland, one taken when the starlet was in her twenties and one taken this week at 70, our crack investigative team has discovered vast differences between the two photos, in terms of hair, skin and body shape.

Confronted with the findings of the Mail investigation, Ms Ekland refused to comment, but a passer-by suggested the differences between the two

photos were the result of her being 50 years older in one of the photos.

Rejecting this explanation, the Mail promised further investigations into what they believe is a sinister plot by women to appear less attractive to men.

On other pages

Mail condemns misogyny towards lovely little ladies on Twitter **94**

CHECK OUT

Nursery Times

Friday, Once-upon-a-time

TROLL ARRESTED UNDER BRIDGE

By our Social Media Staff **Tweetie Pie**

AN EVIL TROLL who had terrorised three innocent billy goats gruff with a constant stream of abuse and invective, was last night in custody having been tracked down to his home underneath the bridge.

The Troll had hidden his identity from the victims by staying underneath the bridge and tweeting them when they trip-trapped across to reach the greener grass on the other side.

The billy goats at first ignored the tweets but when the Troll threatened to attack them and gobble them up, they finally took action and reported the Troll to his mother. The troll who went by the name @goathater immediately apologised before finding another bridge to go and hide under.

PC Plod said, "we are on the case and we are determined to find out once and for all what this Twitter thing is."

On other pages

● Grumpy angry about dwarf happiness survey **4** ● Dr Foster cancels out of hours Gloucester visits due to floods **7** ● Jack Spraatchi divorces wife in record time **12**

ZIMBABWE ELECTION LATEST

by our Harare reporter **Dee Ceased**

African Union election monitors have concluded there were no irregularities in the way that Robert Mugabe and his Zanu PF party rigged Zimbabwe's general election.

"Thousands of dead people across the country voting, the election count taking place three days before the election took place and the announcement that a record 164% of voters had voted for Mugabe was exactly the way we thought Mugabe would steal the election and we were right," said an impartial election monitor taking tea with Robert Mugabe.

"Of course the result is torture for Morgan Tsvangirai and his MDC supporters, but they'll be getting used to plenty more torture in the years to come"

"We must applaud Robert Mugabe that at 89 he's now got a seventh term to add to his six previous terms – dictator, thug, bully, murderer, thief and crook."

The White House expressed concern about the election, saying the MDC should have been allowed to take office for a few months before being ousted by the military and then all their supporters shot like in Eygpt.

ZIMBABWE VOTE RIGGING

A lot of people who voted for you are dead

And the ones who didn't soon will be!

I KNEW IT WAS J.K. ROWLING ALL ALONG

By all books writers on every paper

I COULD tell as soon as I started reading "The Cuckoo's Calling" that it was by a woman, of course. The masterfully realistic descriptions of clutch bags, elite parties and oxidised silver bracelets – they all showed clearly that whoever had written "The Cuckoo's Calling" was a woman and a wealthy one to boot.

My suspicions were further heightened by the clever clue in the author's pen name. "Robert Galbraith" was obviously a reference to Jack Kerouac, who owned a dog called Gall-Breath and had a second cousin named Robert. The "J.K." of "Jack Kerouac" was the clearest

Mystery author

indication yet that J.K. Rowling was the crime debutante who had bent her pen to producing "The Cuckoo's Calling". I had guessed this immediately, of course, but out of respect for Ms Rowling, I said nothing.

There was hard detective work ahead of me, of course, but I was determined to confirm my suspicions one way or another. So when I mentioned on Twitter that the book was quite good and a drunk lawyer's wife tweeted me saying that it was by J.K. Rowling, that provided me with a clue. And so it turned out that my guess had been 100% correct. I had solved the mystery.

Book world stunned as author reveals pseudonym by Our Literary Staff **Mike Fishy**

There was widespread astonishment in the publishing world after little-known author Jeffrey Archer revealed that he had written all the Harry Potter novels under the pseudonym J.K. Rowling.

"The reason I did this was I didn't want my fame as the greatest author in the history of the world, famous for such books as *The Bible, Catch 22* and *Great Expectations,* to influence publishers into buying my books.

"But now the truth is out for all to see. It was me who created the world of the Wizard Dimbleby and life at Simon Hoggarts Academy for Magical Things Happening With Brooms and things like that.

"Now the truth is out, the publishers just need to send me a cheque for the £52 billion I'm owed in royalties, or a prostitute, and that will be the end of the matter."

EGYPT IN FLAMES

Look... the ruins of a once proud civilisation

"We went to Egypt for our holidays"

EGYPT – MILITARY PROMISE TO RESTORE DEMOCRACY

By our Middle East staff, **Nile Ferguson**

The head of the Egyptian military, General Abdul Fattah Assassi Nator, pledged today that democracy would return and be open to every party, from every side of the political spectrum, just as soon as his troops had killed everyone who might vote for the Muslim Brotherhood's Mohammed Morsi.

"We're committed to free and fair elections for anyone still living," he explained, while lobbing a grenade into a nearby mosque.

A spokesman for the Muslim Brotherhood was unavailable for comment, as he was dead.

MINISTER JUSTIFIES SOARING RAIL FARES

by Our Transport Staff **Phil Carriages and Stan Dingroomonly**

Millions of commuters – most of them on the 7.35 from Haslemere to Waterloo – were yesterday incandescent at being told that their rail fares would yet again be rising by well over the rate of inflation.

But Transport Secretary Patrick McWhohe *(subs – please check name)* was last night quick to defend the hike, which will raise the cost of a season ticket between Peterborough and Kings Cross to an eye-watering £47,000 a year.

"These increases," he said, "are essential to maintain the efficiency of our rail service.

We need to fund the massive investment programme required to keep our directors' bonuses at a competitive level."

Totally Unfare

"It is only by putting in a record level of funding that we can ensure that the bonuses arrive regularly and on time.

"It is only if we give top priority to paying our senior staff the kind of money they are asking for that they will be able to afford a season ticket from Peterborough to Kings Cross, or possibly to buy the kind of car which will enable them to avoid having to catch the 7.35 from Haslemere to Waterloo."

Nursery Times

································ Friday, In Times Long Past ································

PRINCE'S SECRET LOBBYING REVEALED

By Our Political Correspondent, **Michael Whiterabbit**

DETAILS have emerged of the extensive interference in Nurseryland Government by Prince Charmless.

The Prince of Never-Never-Going-To-Be-King-Land has huge amounts of spare time in which to write pompous letters and arrange irritating meetings with officialdom. Issues especially close to his heart include:

● the effects of climate change and whether or not the sky is going to fall on his head

● genetically modified crops and the threat to Nurseryland of giants climbing down the resultant beanstalks

● modern architecture, showing his preference for traditional shoes to house old women with too many children, as opposed to concrete tower blocks

● the construction of Wind-farms in the Willows, to capitalise on the Big Bad Wolf's huffing and puffing

● country pursuits, such as Fantastic Mr Fox-hunting.

Said one Government source, the Crooked Man, "Once upon a time, a long, long time ago, we might have been interested in what Prince Charmless had to say, but now we just wish he would shut up, so we can all live happily ever after."

On other pages

● Humpty Dumpty throws himself at Ed Tweedledum **4** ● Fat Controller to grow 4.1% fatter following rail fares increase **10** ● Jack and Jill to impose £29 surcharge to fetch pail of water **16**.

Fracking Latest

"What a relief! – I thought they said Cuadrilla was coming to ruin our village, but it's only Godzilla!"

RUSSIA BANS GAY IMAGERY

The Kremlin has confirmed that the following blatantly "butch" photos have been banned for fear they will inflame homosexual urges amongst Russia's youth...

 ## Daily Tudorgraph

— 1587, Friday —

Fleet Sails On 'Routine Exercise' Off Ye Spanish Coast

by Our Naval Correspondent MARY ROSE

Cheering crowds yesterday bade farewell to Vice Admiral Sir Francis Drake, as he led a Royal Naval task force out of Portsmouth on what was officially described as no more than a "friendly routine visit to the coast of Spain".

Only here for the Beard

A spokesman for Her Majesty Queen Elizabeth's government was quick to insist that Drake's voyage was in no way intended as a provocative response to recent belligerent statements from the Spanish capital Madrid.

Said the spokesman, "Operation Beardsinge," as it has been dubbed, "was planned months ago, long before these dago Johnnies got up to their silly games over Her Majesty's rightful possession of Gibraltar.

"Sir Francis and his fleet have absolutely no intention of sailing into Cadiz harbour and setting fire to the entire Spanish fleet.

"His orders are merely to sail into Spanish waters in a perfectly peaceful fashion — and, if this reminds that paella-guzzling, Rioja-swilling, bunch of donkey torturers not to mess with John Bull and Her Majesty's loyal subjects in Gibraltar and the Falklands, so be it."

Late score from Cadiz

England — 37 galleons destroyed

Spain — 0

New Faces of M&S Unveiled

MARKS & SPENCER proudly announced the line-up for their new advertising campaign yesterday.

"These people are a mixture of fashion icons, athletes and miscellaneous celebrities, but they have one thing in common; they are all at the top of their relative professions, be they controversial piss artists or play actors," said an excitable spokesperson.

Doubts have been raised that any of the individuals pictured actually wear M&S but these are hotly denied. "Crikey, of course I do," said one, "or is that S&M?"

GIBRALTAR SHOCK

Wow – Britain still has a warship!

"It's good to see the High Street coming back to life"

From The Message Boards

Members of the online community respond to the major issues of the day...

England cricketers apologise

Guys, I see the England players have said sorry for their "inappropriate" celebrations at the Oval. Seems they had a party on the field after the final test, and around midnight a few of them splashed the old boots on the hallowed square! As luck would have it an Aussie reporter spotted them and made his own "splash" in the papers down under! Ray Illingworth reckons the boys defiled the historic turf, but I can't see the harm in a good old-fashioned sticky wicket! – *Bogbrush*

England won the Slashes! ☺ lol! – *Danny Daz*

and the england lady's won the gashes ☺ – *hatfield gooner*

What a shower! No pees for the wicket! – *Twelfth Man*

fare play 2 are boy's no sign of the aussie's they must of gone off 4 bad lite – *eltham john*

shame monty wernt there to join in after he pissed on them bouncer's in brighton ☺ hes a good roll model cos he show's muslim's can be like normel peple – *Hunny pot*

It's times like this that one misses dear old Brian Johnson's schoolboy humour. Imagine what fun he would have had with this! I still chuckle at his legendary TMS commentary, "the bowler's Holding, the batsman's Willey"! – *Father Time*

woud of bin funnyer if he said the bowler's holdin batmans nob – *Darling Deneyze*

The journalist concerned is a certain Mr Conn, an apt name for a citizen of that benighted convict colony if ever there was one. He claims to have witnessed events from the "overflow areas" of the press box, which suggests that he and his unappetising colleagues would do well to examine their own habits before leaping to criticise others. – *Gerard*

I doubt Mr Conn was complaining when the Foster's Oval was named after Australian piss. – *Craigspist*

Try any of that at the MCG this Christmas and they'll end up on crutches like Bogbrush did last time he was down under. – *King of the Hill*

G'day Kingy! – *Bogbrush*

Go fuck yourself dipshit. – *King of the Hill*

Jacob Rees Mogg 'unaware of organisation's politics'

JACOB REES MOGG has insisted he had no idea of the Ku Klux Klan's politics when he accepted an invitation to speak at their annual barn dance and cross burning in Tennessee.

"Some might call me naïve, but all I could see was a group of agreeable chaps who enjoy dressing up in white and riding through the countryside burning down buildings," insisted a contrite Mr Rees Mogg.

"I can assure my party that I won't be making this mistake ever again – a point I will make very clear in a speech I'm giving at the Hitler Youth's Annual Dinner Dance and Beetle Drive in Crawley next month."

Traditional Britain Group

EYE SPORT

CRICKET NEWS

Australia 'Picked Wrong Team'

The Australian selectors have come in for vitriolic criticism from the local media for their team selection.

"Those drongos definitely picked the wrong team to win this series," thundered a furious Sydney Morning Herald editorial. "They should have picked the 1993 team – Border, Taylor, Shane Warne, Hayden, Boon and Hughes would have walked this series."

– PILBROW –
Hot spot

I HATE YOU!

I HATE YOU!

Post-nuptial agreement

Mary isn't the only beard to get abuse on Twitter

ME AND MY SPOON

JEREMY PAXMAN

Jeremy, I know you've been in this column before because you are a national treasure...

Oh, come off it...

No, let me finish. Recent events have rather put you back in the news, so I wanted to ask you if beards have played a major part in your life?

This is ridiculous. I came to talk about a really serious subject, namely spoons. I regard spoons as a very important issue and I...

No, Jeremy, I'm sorry to interrupt, but how long do you intend to keep this interesting new addition to your chin...

This is utterly preposterous. I came here to have an intelligent discussion about an important item of cutlery, and all you can talk about is facial hair...

Just answer the question. Are you going to shave or not?

I really don't think that this line of enquiry is leading anywhere.

Yes or no, Mr Paxman...

I'm sorry, I'm not going to dignify this matter with a...

Come on, it's a simple question. Just answer it.

I've never been treated like this in my life. I'm not standing for this any longer.

Come back, Mr Paxman, I had one more question to ask you. Has anything amusing ever happened to you with a beard? Mr Paxman... *(at this point the interview was terminated)*

LATEST LATEST BABY LATEST

What the baby panda might look like, if it's like any other panda cub

By Our Celebrity Baby Staff, Matt Ernity

In a frenetic few weeks for the world's baby media, news crews have gathered yet again to speculate on another imminent baby birth.

A media circus has appeared outside the panda cage at Edinburgh zoo, while over-excited journalists have been maintaining a 24-hour vigil waiting for the cub to arrive sometime next month. Well-wishers have been passing flowers through the cage which the grateful pandas have eaten.

Panda-monium

Said one journalist, "It's the most exciting baby event since the one we over-hyped last week. This is the most amazing celebrity baby until we get onto Jordan's. The question now is whether the pandas are middle-class enough to marry."

Rumours of the panda's pregnancy started to spread when a number of telltale signs were spotted. The female panda developed a craving for bamboo and it was suggested that her brain had gone to mush. Also she had got very irritable, stopped drinking wine, redecorated her cage, given up her book club and was now denying her partner sex.

Experts say they won't know for sure that the pandas are pregnant until the Middleton's Partypieces range of baby panda party accessories becomes available.

WHAT WILL THEY CALL THE BABY PANDA?

Yuan Yuan • Yawn Yawn • **Hu Kares** • Ping Pong • **Wiff Waff** • Boris • **Kung Fu Panda** • Kung Fu Panda 2 • **Gang Nam** • Psy • **Psymon Cowell** • George Alexander Louis (*That's enough panda names. Ed.*)

"You're not to disturb Papa for at least 15 minutes. He's taking a selfie"

EGGED MILIBAND

Hooray! Someone knows who I am!

Cardinals Prepare Popemobile As Pope Francis Arrives On Copacabana Beach

URGENT BABY APPEAL

By His Royal Highness the Duke of Cambridge

Do you have ten pounds to spare?

Then, please, please don't spend it on the Royal baby. Kate and I have been inundated with literally thousands of useless and unwanted presents already. And, to be honest, it's unlikely that baby George is ever going to want for anything anyway. So please dig deep into your hearts and help us find a home for the following items:

● A tree from Ed Miliband. Thanks, Ed, but I think there are probably quite enough in Hyde Park as it is.

● *A packet of coffee from Nick Clegg. Bless you, Nick, but we've got something keeping us awake all night already.*

● Two dozen signed copies of *Celebrate – a guide to how to throw a party* by Pippa Middleton. Thanks, Pippa, but you already gave us two dozen copies for Christmas.

● *A billion teddy bears. Thanks, public, George has probably got enough now.*

● Boujis life membership card – thanks but no thanks, Harry.

● *Weight Watchers Kit. Thank you, but 8 lbs 6 oz isn't that heavy for a baby, Aunt Fergie.*

● One double-barrelled shotgun. Thanks, Gramps, but he cried all the way through the Glorious Twelfth.

So why not adopt a Royal gift today? You can do so simply by driving to Kensington Palace and loading up your 4x4 from the skip you'll find just next door to Harry's bottle bank.

OBAMA PAYS TRIBUTE TO KING

I have a drone

EXCLUSIVE TO ALL NEWSPAPERS
MARTIN LUTHER KING'S DREAM – HAS IT BEEN REALISED?

No.

King's 'I Have A Dream' Speech Recalled

by Our Money Staff **Bill Cash** and **Ezra Pound**

It is now 50 days since Mervyn Luther King made what has come to be looked back on as the most historic and iconic speech of our time.

Before a crowd of 50,000 financial journalists from all over he world, he pronounced, "I have a dream. A dream of a country that is in the black. A country which no longer owes £1.2 trillion to its creditors. A country that has no need to print imaginary money, to lend to the banks, so that they can pay interest on it to the government, so the government can pretend that it is reducing its deficit."

"I have a dream," said the Reverend Former Governor of the Bank of England, "that in our lifetime we may see a country of high growth, low inflation and happy smiling people of all races, confident that they will be able to get a job, and not have to live on benefits paid for by the Government out of all that money it has been having to borrow.

"Will we see this in my lifetime?" thundered the legendary orator of Threadneedle Street.

"Probably not", he concluded as he stepped down from his post.

"Geoffrey lives in his own private hell"

DRAWING ALL FAITHS TOGETHER

THE CASE FOR WAR
by Our Life President, the Rev. Tony Blair

Hi!

All over the world decent people are gazing in horror at the tragic events unfolding in the unhappy country of Syria.

And everywhere we hear the cry going up, "Something must be done". Even here, in the Mediterranean port of Ambre Solaire, where I am staying on the superyacht "Oligarski III", on which I am an honoured guest, that cry has become deafening.

And, as the world's foremost spiritual leader, I am aware that millions of ordinary folk are looking to me at this time to give the world the moral lead that it so desperately craves.

But I am also, of course, the world's most experienced living statesman, which means that I can not only give to the world a spiritual lead – I can also draw on everything I learned from our successful interventions in Iraq and Afghanistan to give our current leaders down-to-earth, pragmatic and realistic practical advice.

The solution to the immensely complex problem posed to the world by the actions of the Syrian dictator is, in fact, astonishingly simple.

And it can be spelled out in two simple words. BOMB SYRIA!

No doubt, the fainthearts will object and ask, "But what about the Russians? Surely they won't be too pleased if we attack their ally Mr Assad?". But, I say the answer to that is equally simple. BOMB RUSSIA!

And, if the same lily-livered whingers then try to point out that Mr Assad has got other allies, such as the Iranians, Hezbollah and the Chinese and that it is possible they might also cause us a bit of trouble, I say again the answer could not be simpler. BOMB IRAN. BOMB HEZBOLLAH. BOMB CHINA. BOMB EVERYONE!

This is my way to bring peace to Syria and indeed the entire Islamic world of the Middle East.

And I say that with all the authority of a man whose tough and decisive actions brought lasting peace to both Iraq and Afghanistan.

The time has come for an end to all this hand-wringing – hands must be put to work to get covered in blood.

As I said to my host, the Emir of Bakhanda, on the last yacht I was staying on when I was leading multi-faith prayers before cocktails, "Blessed are the peacemakers, for they shall make war".

The Emir humorously replied to me, "And, Tony, they shall also make money!".

How right he was and how wise!

Yours,

Rev. T. Blair

Chief Executive, D.A.F.T. (former vicar of St. Albion's)

WHY SYRIA IS NOT LIKE IRAQ

That historic Cameron speech in full

"Simple moral choice... chemical weapons... UN weapons inspectors on the ground... convincing dossier from the Joint Intelligence Committee... legal opinion from Attorney General... UN resolution not essential... no desire for regime change... well aware of mission creep... intervention will help stop terrorism... dangerous not to intervene... not rushing into it just because the Americans say so... precision strikes... minimal collateral damage... I'm a really straight kind of a guy... it'll be fine or my name's not Tony Blair."

Tales from the Bible...
THE ROAD TO DAMASCUS

BY ST PAUL JOHNSON
(WITH HELP FROM ST MATTHEW PARRIS AND ST JOHN HUMPHRYS)

AND AT THAT time, there was a man called Dave who was preaching about the evils of the Syrians and trying to persuade the people to follow him.

And as he was going down the road of bombing Damascus he was suddenly hit by a blinding flash and lo he did hear the voice of Common Sense coming out of the heavens. And the voice said "Dave, Dave, why are you doing this?" And Dave was frankly stumped for an answer and was struck dumb and blind, but mainly dumb. He

fell to the ground and then did a complete U-turn, walking back down the road, away from Damascus, a chastened man.

And from that time onwards, people looked on him in a different light and no longer called him by the name Dave, but by a new name – Idiot.

SYRIA CRISIS ESCALATES

Where do you stand on chemical weapons?

My favourite is polonium

Numéro 94
Le High-Level Diplomacie!

President Hollande *(pour c'est lui)*: Bonjour, Monsieur Barack! Nous sommes vos new friends, dans un nouveau relationship speciale. No more fromage-munching, surrender-singes! Nous sommes les gung-ho interventionists, que vous pouvez rely on.

President Obama *(sur le telephone)*: I'm sorry, I've got someone on the other line.

President Hollande: Vous n'avez besoin de parler avec anyone else. Forget le UN! Forget le Council de Securité! Forget le NATO! La France stands épaule à épaule avec les Americaines. Liberté, fraternité, et illegalité!!!! When do nous commencer le bombing? *(Il burst out into chanson)* Allons enfants de la patrie, le Beaujolais nouveau est arrivé!

President Obama: I'm terribly sorry, I'll have to put you on hold, it's my good friend Mr Cameron...

President Hollande: Non non non, il n'est pas votre ami! Les rosbifs sont deeply unreliable, unlike nous. Monsieur Obama, Monsieur Obama?

(Forty minutes plus tard...)

President Obama: President Hollande, having talked it through with my British friend, I think I'm going to delay things for a while.

President Hollande: Quoi?! Vous n'est pas serious?

President Obama: You're going to have to go it alone.

President Hollande: Sacré bleu! Ooh la la! Zut alors! Merde! This est mon Waterloo!

© *The late Miles Kington, 2013.*

Kinnock – 'How dare they say Miliband is Labour's worst ever leader?'
That supportive speech

" I am totally, utterly and utterly, totally appalled, disgusted and outraged by the suggestion I see being made on every side that Ed Miliband is proving to be a total, utter and totally utter disaster as the leader of the Labour Party.

There are even those who are idiotic enough to be suggesting that Mr Miliband is the worst leader that Labour has ever had. This, in my view, is utterly, totally, totally, utterly and utterly, totally wrong.

As everyone who has made even the most casual, cursory and superficial study of British politics would know, there is only one man whose grasp of political issues, whose sense of strategy and whose interminable oratorical windbagging have given him the undisputed claim to have been the most utterly, utterly and totally, totally useless leader either of the Labour Party or, indeed, possibly any other party at any time in history.

And that man, I can state without undue modesty and without fear of contradiction, is myself. "

© *The Rt Hon the Lord Kinnock of Flanelly, 2013.*

HOW COMPUTERS HAVE CHANGED

Kerry announcement on Syria

IN a major speech today from under a table in a bar in Romford, Kerry Katona lashed out at Syria.

"I hate her, Syria is the worst... she's worse than that slag Jordan... I hope she gets what she deserves or somefin and is the first to get voted out of the Big Brother house, whoever she is... that slag stole my boyfriend or my drugs or she disspected my children or somefin... yeah, that Syria, wot a total bitch...

(Reuters)

SYRIA — WHO CAN STOP THIS MAD MAN?

Everybody knows I never support strikes

NEW OLD LYRICS 1

The PM wants to fight,
But by jingo if we do:
We've got no men,
We've got no guns,
We've got no money too.

(MacDermott's War Song, 1877)

'American Spring' spreads

by Our Washington Correspondent
Dee Mockracy

HUGE crowds spilled out onto the streets of cities throughout the Middle East last night declaring that the American Spring was well and truly underway, with democracy taking hold in backwards countries where it was thought long since dead.

"All around the West, crazed tyrannical leaders are giving their powers to long-forgotten publicly elected bodies, because they haven't a clue what to do about Syria," said one swarthy man, shooting bullets into the air.

"If this continues, we could see democracies flowering across Britain, France and the US."

Amid the euphoria, some voices urged caution. "The American people are historically very comfortable with being ruled by an insane religious leader, happy to bomb, maim and kill at a moment's notice without his authority ever being questioned," warned Donald Rumsfeld.

"Just because democracy is all the rage in the Middle East that doesn't mean it will transfer successfully here."

"The dawning of the American Spring is wonderful news for those of us in the Middle East who treasure democracy," declared a smiling President Assad, as he joined in celebrations with fireworks and Sarin gas canisters going off on the streets of Damascus.

"This means I'm the only leader allowed to bomb his people without having to ask permission first."

FROST/GOD
THE INTERVIEW

FROST: God, you've had an extraordinary career. You're omniscient, you're omnipresent, you're omnipotent. A bit like me.

GOD: Hahahahhaha....

FROST: But seriously, I'd like to start right back at the beginning...

GOD: Well, there was the Word...

(Interview continues for the next 100 million hours, until Frost pounces with his killer question)

FROST: Would you like to apologise to the people of the world for the existence of Evil?

GOD: *(pause)* Well... it was actually a question of free will for mankind, but...

(Silence. God sweats)

FROST: Are you going to apologise?

(Silence. God sweats some more)

FROST: Because if you don't apologise, you may regret it for all eternity?

(Silence. God cracks)

GOD: I let down my friends, I let down the universe.

(Frost doesn't notice greatest coup in interviewing history)

FROST: And what's your favourite colour?

GOD: I don't know, white?

FROST: God, thank you very much.

TW3 MAN DEAD

He was a great loss to satire...

...Yes, he provided material for satirists for 50 years

POETRY CORNER

**In Memoriam
Sir David Frost,
legendary broadcaster**

So. Farewell
Then David Frost,
Satirist, interviewer
And friend to
The Stars.

It was unkindly
Said that you
"Rose without trace".
Now you have risen
Even higher.

E.J. Thribbute
(17½ pages in every newspaper)

That BBC Syrian Debate
What You Missed

Paxman: Welcome to our War Special. With me in the studio is some madman who's opposed to intervening immediately. Mr Woolly, don't you feel ashamed of yourself?

Woolly: Good evening, Jeremy. Nice beard, by the way. I just feel that a moment's reflection may be necessary before we...

Paxman: Have you seen these pictures from a forthcoming Panorama?

Woolly: Yes, I have. You're showing them quite a lot on the BBC.

Paxman: Does this moving footage of dead children not make it blindingly obvious, even to someone as callous and inhuman as you, that we should launch a missile attack at once instead of standing idly by?

Woolly: No, it is appalling, obviously, but I think there is a rational argument to be made about the practical effects of any intervention at this point and also a moral discussion to be had about...

Paxman: Oh come off it, Mr Woolly! You've got blood on your hands. President Assad will be watching this programme and laughing.

Woolly: Mostly at your beard, Jeremy.

Radio

Gardeners' Question Time
BBC Radio 4

Eric Robson, Bob Flowerdew, Chris Beardshaw and Bunny Guinness are joined by celebrity guest Cheryl Cole who needs the panel's help with an embarrassing outbreak of greenfly on her rosebush.

EYE RATING: *Mulch ado about nothing.*

THE SAD TALE OF MR BROCK AND MRS TIGGY-WINKLE
BY BEATRIX POTTER

ONCE UPON A TIME there was a friendly little hedgehog called Mrs Tiggy-Winkle. She was loved by all the other animals because she was so sweet and good-natured.

For the Flopsy Bunnies she would iron their little pocket handkerchiefs. For Mrs Jemima Puddleduck she washed her pretty scarf. For Mr Jeremy Fisher she would dry-clean his smart waistcoat whenever he fell into the pond (which was quite often!).

But there was just one creature of whom Mrs Tiggy-Winkle was very frightened.

It wasn't that Mr Brock the Badger didn't like her. He liked hedgehogs only too much – for his dinner.

One day, Mrs Tiggy-Winkle's friend Tom Kitten came to her little home to get his furry gloves washed, and what did he find?

He found Mr Brock finishing the last morsels of poor Mrs Tiggy-Winkle.

"You wicked, horrid badger," said Tom. "You'll be punished for this."

The only reply Mr Brock could manage was to burst into a terrible fit of coughing.

"Are you ill?" asked Tom Kitten, frightened by the wheezing noise that was coming from the badger's chest.

But before Mr Brock could utter another sound, there was a loud bang and he fell backwards, stone dead.

Then Mr McGregor, the farmer, appeared with his shotgun.

"That's another one gone," he said.

And all the animals cried, "Hurrah for Mr McGregor. At last our friends the hedgehogs will be safe again from their worst enemy".

And do you know what the moral of this story is, children?

That's right – that the animal world is more complicated than some people would have you believe, and it does not lend itself to sentimental anthropomorphism.

© Princess Beatrice of Potter (surely Beatrix of the Netherlands? Ed.)

How Do You Know When You're Middle-Aged?

Those ten tell-tale signs...

1 You don't understand what young peasants are talking about.

2 You struggle to read Chaucer in weak candlelight.

3 You hate rowdy taverns.

4 You constantly worry that you might have the Black Death.

5 You don't know or care who Blondel is sleeping with.

6 You tell your wife that Crusaders seem to look younger every year.

7 You struggle with new technology such as the heavy plough and the longbow.

8 You find Gothic architecture too modern.

9 You keep forgetting who the King is.

10 You dream of buying a second hovel in France

(That's enough Middle Ages, Ed.)

Those OED New Words in Full

Journalists all over Britain were rushing last night to fill up their newspapers with a list of new words to be included in the online edition of the Oxford English Dictionary.

Here are just a few of them:

TWERK, *verb*. To issue a press release knowing that journalists are not prepared to do any "work" in August and will print the handout in full.

SELFIE, *noun*. Word used to describe an organisation which goes out of its way to promote its "self" by issuing press releases in August to journalists too lazy to do anything other than put them straight into the paper.

PHABLET, *noun*. Belief of newspaper editors that anything to do with iPhones, Tablets and the digital world in general is so important and exciting that it merits huge coverage in their pages, even if the story is quite obviously a "selfie" and quite blatantly "twerking" (*see above*).

GO HOME OR FACE ARREST

PRIVATE EYE

No. 1345
26 July –
8 August 2013
£1.50

WOMAN HAS BABY

INSIDE: Some other stuff

22 July 2013